Teresa's Man

DAMODAR MAUZO is a novelist, short-fiction writer, literary critic and scriptwriter. His works include the short-story collections *Chit'tarangi* (for children), *Ganthan*, *Zagrannam*, *Rumadful* and *Bhurghim Mhugelim Tim*; the novellas *Sood*, *Tsunami Simon* and *Ek Ashil'lo Babulo* (for children); the novel *Karmelin* (recipient of the Sahitya Akademi Award 1983); and the biographical sketches *Oshe Ghodle Shenoy Goembab* and *Unch Haves Unch Mathem*. He wrote the screenplay for the National Award-winning film, *Aleesha*, as well as dialogues for two more films.

Co-founder and curator of the Goa Art and Literature Festival, Damodar Mauzo also serves as a member of the jury for the Saraswati Samman, one of India's premier literary awards. He is also an adviser to the Samanvay Festival, organized by India Habitat Centre, New Delhi. Part of many national-level literary organizations, Mauzo is widely recognized for his integrity, social activism and his commitment to literature.

XAVIER COTA, teacher, former banker, and sports administrator, translates fiction and non-fiction from Konkani to English. His translations and articles have been featured in *The Week*, *Gentleman*, *Man's World*, *See Goa* and *Katha Prize Stories* as well as in publications brought out by the Sahitya Akademi. He has previously translated two works by Damodar Mauzo: a collection of short stories, *These Are My Children*; and the novella, *Tsunami Simon*.

Teresa's Man

and other stories from Goa

DAMODAR MAUZO

Translated from the Konkani by

Xavier Cota

RUPA

Published by
Rupa Publications India Pvt. Ltd 2014
7/16, Ansari Road, Daryaganj
New Delhi 110002

Sales centres:
Allahabad Bengaluru Chennai
Hyderabad Jaipur Kathmandu
Kolkata Mumbai

ISBN: 978-81-291-3466-0

10 9 8 7 6 5 4 3 2 1

First impression 2014

Typeset in Dante MT by SÜRYA, New Delhi
Printed by Thomson Press India Ltd. Faridabad

Contents

From the Mouths of Babes

Mithila had been irritated from the day before. The only day in the entire week which had a silver lining was Juma, Friday, the weekly off. It had been wasted yesterday. And, now, Babu had not yet returned from school.

It was the Muthawa, the omnipresent religious police, who had screwed up Juma the previous day. What was it today? Was Rajesh delayed in collecting Babu from kindergarten? Did news from Germany hold Rajesh up? Perhaps he was caught in traffic. Or maybe he'd been detained, like yesterday, by the Muthawa—perhaps by the civil police, the Surta, this time.

Yesterday, while leaving the house, their mood had been so bubbly! Rajesh had been in his element. If there had been one irritant, it had been the burqa. But, by now, she had taken that in her stride. Was there an alternative? In Saudi Arabia, and especially in Riyadh, a woman just could not go out unless she was wearing one.

Mithila loved to sit by Rajesh's side as he drove. After six days of being cooped up in the house, Juma was her day of freedom. In carrying on a conversation, even as she wore the enveloping outer garment, Mithila had felt that a

1

curtain had fallen between them. She just had not been able to stand it. But, inside the car, she knew that she could lift the veil of the burqa. This had made her happy.

Even though it was Juma, Rajesh had turned the car towards his office. His own company had interviewed him online for a research fellowship. The results should have been out by now. A worried Rajesh had entered his office. Booting his computer, he'd clicked open his inbox. There was mail for him from Jeddah, Kuwait, the US and even one from Germany. All routine stuff. The message he was expecting wasn't there. Disappointed, he'd logged out, left the office, and got into the car.

'Nothing yet?' Mithila had asked.

'No.'

'No problem. It may come tomorrow. They haven't taken anybody else, have they?'

'Who knows? They might have.'

Changing the subject along with the gears, he'd asked, 'First we go to Batha, right?'

Getting down at the market, they'd stocked up on masalas, papads and desiccated coconut. After wandering around for some time, they had entered the Al Rashid Super Market. This store was like a fair. Articles of various descriptions beckoned and Babu, too, enjoyed himself here. Suddenly, Mithila's attention was drawn to a T-shirt—cream-coloured, with a mellow-green collar, and laces instead of buttons. Mithila had impulsively grabbed Rajesh's hand and tugged at it. Lifting the shirt, she'd placed it against Rajesh's body, urging him to buy it. An

Arab standing to their left had stepped forward. Flashing an ID at Rajesh, he'd proclaimed that he was a Muthawa and asked for Rajesh's Akama. Rajesh's identity card carried a photograph of him along with Mithila and Babu. After looking closely at the photograph and at Mithila, the Arab had satisfied himself that she was indeed Rajesh's wife. Speaking in Arabic, he'd sternly told Rajesh, 'Your wife does not know to behave properly. Tell her that holding a man's hand and being familiar with him in public is against our rules. We will have to take action against her. This is the first warning. A repetition of the offence will mean that both, no, all three of you will have to be deported. You understand?'

Rajesh had apologized in Arabic. The T-shirt was forgotten.

'Let's go, Mithu,' Rajesh had croaked. Mithila thought that Rajesh had unnecessarily become nervous. As soon as they sat in the car, Mithila had burst out heatedly, 'Damn these people and their stone-age rules!'

'And despite knowing this, you publicly grabbed my hand?' Rajesh had countered.

Mithila was hurt. 'Was it a sin to hold my own husband's hand?'

'But you know that it's not permitted here, don't you?'

'I know. As if they don't touch their wives' hands!'

'They do. But they don't make a public spectacle of it. I've told you a thousand times. Here we have to behave within *their* moral confines.'

The argument would have gone on, but Babu, who all

this while had uncomprehendingly watched the proceedings in silence, had become uncomfortable as they both raised their voices. He had begun to sob. Abandoning their plans to have lunch at the Holiday Drive Inn, Rajesh had turned the car around and headed back to their apartment.

Rajesh was quick to anger but equally quick to cool down. By evening, he had been ready to go out again, but Mithila was still annoyed. She wasn't angry with the Muthawa—he was only doing his job. He had issued the warning after seeing her behaviour. But why did *this* guy have to get mad at his wife? Arabs wrap their women up in burqas and hijabs and don't touch them in public. True. But the whole world knows how they behave with women away from the public eye! Rajesh didn't like my pulling his hand in the supermarket. Fine. But couldn't he have hugged me after getting home at least? Mithila had sat in front of the TV, stewing silently.

But, after dinner, Babu had insisted that he wanted an ice cream. She felt like telling Rajesh to take Babu and go out, but then she, too, went along.

Slipping the garment over her nightie, Mithila sat in the car with her face veiled, in dumb silence. Even in the ice cream parlour, the burqa remained firmly in place.

'Lift up the veil now!' Rajesh had said, but Mithila did not move.

He bought three cones. Giving one to Babu, he held out to Mithila. To make it obvious that she was avoiding contact, Mithila received it gingerly with two fingers.

Rajesh burst out laughing. Mithila, too, laughed behind her veil. But, to emphasize that she was still angry, she turned her back on him, lifted the veil, and started on her cone.

Babu was entering his fifth year, but he still insisted on sleeping between his parents. By the time they'd put him to bed with fairytales, it was eleven. Sensing that Mithila was getting drowsy, Rajesh had shut the book he was reading and switched off the bedside lamp. Mithila's hand was on Babu's shoulder. When Rajesh's hand touched Mithila's, she did not react. His hand crept slowly upwards.

'So, *now* it's permissible to touch!' Mithila had remarked.

'Enough of that. When have I ever stopped you from touching me when we are alone?' Rajesh had asked in a soothing tone. 'As long as we are here in Saudi, let's patiently bear these restrictions. Tomorrow, if we reach Germany, who will bother us?' Rajesh had gently pulled her towards him.

'Babu is here,' Mithila had said, resisting Rajesh.

'He's fast asleep. Now I'm your king and you are my queen.' Rajesh had vaulted over Babu and squeezed in by Mithila's side.

'Now I'm your king and you are my queen'. Rajesh had spoken these very words six years ago when they were on their honeymoon in Mahabaleshwar.

Mithila had been very happy to have the handsome, capable engineer as her husband. Adding to that pleasure was the cool, pleasant, hill-station atmosphere of Mahabaleshwar. They'd stayed at a beautiful three-star resort. It had been lovely.

When they had gone out for a stroll in the evening, they had been astounded by the crowds. Since it was May, the height of the Indian summer, the hotels in this hill station had been overflowing with holiday-makers from the plains. They had even come across quite a few acquaintances from Goa in the crowd. The ambience was so pleasant! A cool gentle breeze wafted over them and Mithila had impulsively clasped her hand round Rajesh's arm and gently pulled him towards her.

Rajesh had sprung apart with an instinctive start. Disentangling his arm, he glanced around almost guiltily. 'People are watching us. Don't hold on to me like this,' Rajesh had said to her in a subdued, almost bashful voice.

Mithila had looked on at him in wonder. 'What's wrong with my holding your arm?' she'd asked, feeling defeated, 'we're on our honeymoon.'

'It's not that. But in front of everyone...' Rajesh had lamely petered off.

'I'm your legally wedded wife,' Mithila had said, gently pinching him on the arm.

'True, sweetheart, who's denying it? But why do we have to advertise the fact to all and sundry? Let's behave like we do back home in Goa.'

Mithila did not want to start an argument, so she kept quiet. But she found no merit in his viewpoint. As they walked on, they saw half a dozen couples walking hand in hand, glued to one another or with their arms around their shoulders. And each time Mithila made it a point to draw Rajesh's attention. 'Look at *them*!'

'You look at them! I'll show you when we get back to our room!' Rajesh had retorted, laughing.

And, true to his words, as soon as they had entered the room and bolted the door, he'd gathered Mithila in his arms and, hugging her tight, he had said, 'Now I am your king and you are my queen.'

Throughout the honeymoon, Rajesh had been a caring lover, overwhelming Mithila with love and happiness.

But, yes. Even in that happiness, a tiny grain was missing.

They'd gone for an ice cream in the gathering dusk of Mahabaleshwar. Rajesh chose a cocktail ice cream, while Mithila asked for a chocobar.

'What rubbish! I thought it would be good!' Rajesh grimaced, disappointed with his cocktail.

'The chocobar's good. Here, try it.' Mithila held out her ice cream to his mouth.

'No! It isn't hygienic to eat from one another's mouth. You have it,' said Rajesh, curling his mouth in distaste.

Mithila was miffed. 'Your wife's mouth, unhygienic? That's great! It's perfectly fine for an Indian wife to eat from her husband's plate after he has finished, but anything from her mouth is unclean for him!'

'Of course not! Unclean is unclean. Even at home, I object to Mother eating from Father's plate. It's definitely unhygienic.'

That night, in Rajesh's arms, Mithila was aching for Rajesh to kiss her. She had even contemplated taking the initiative, because she had a strong desire to kiss him full on his lips. But recalling the spat they'd had earlier, Mithila had decided: some other time perhaps, and had curbed her desire.

The new generation takes its cues for love and romance from Hindi and English cinema. But Mithila's fascination with kissing had not been inspired by films. Firmly padlocked in her treasure-chest of memories was one incident which sometimes tried to jump out. And it was then, when that desire made itself felt, that she felt a burning desire for Rajesh to kiss her in that way.

It was an old memory. Mithila had just written her SSC High School exam. Her father had some work in Bombay and Mithila had decided to accompany him to the city to see the sights. They'd stayed with her maternal uncle at Dadar. Her cousin Kishor was studying at the prestigious Indian Institute of Technology in Powai. His mother had told him several times to show Mithila around Bombay. Citing his lectures as an excuse, Kishor had declined. Her aunt had taken her around a little, and that had been it for Mithila. But on Saturday afternoon, upon Uncle's insistence, Kishor had taken her to see the Nehru Planetarium at Worli. It was the first time that Mithila had been out alone with a boy. Her heart was thudding with trepidation and, at the same time, she was excited.

Kishor was good-looking and intelligent. They had sat beneath the planetarium dome side by side. She had been overwhelmed with the feeling that she was sitting with a boy on a dark night below an open sky. Kishor was pointing out, his mouth close to her ear, the different constellations in the sky. When I get married, I will travel with my husband this way and he, too, will whisper in my ears like this. Mithila had tingled with the thought. On the way home, with the excuse of crossing the road, Kishor had held her hand a couple of times. Kishor had such an easygoing nature that the reserve which had sprung up between them as they left the house had completely disappeared by the time they returned. Nobody was home, so Kishor had opened the door with his spare key.

Parched by the summer heat, Kishor had asked for water. When Mithila had placed a tumbler of water before him, Kishor had caught her hand along with the tumbler. Gently, he had drawn Mithila close. Before she could decide whether she enjoyed being in his arms or not, he had hugged her. They could feel one another's breath. Involuntarily, Mithila's lips had parted. And in the next moment, Kishor's lips had kissed Mithila's. She experienced an unusual sensation. A strange desire gripped her... Tongue probed tongue when, all of a sudden, they heard the front door being unlatched.

Both of them had sprung apart. Reacting as if nothing had happened, Kishor had picked the glass up and walked out of the room, sipping from it nonchalantly. But Mithila had been thoroughly shaken by the experience. The unwitting feeling that she had committed a grave error had made her nervous. She had been furious with Kishor. And even though her uncle and aunt had pleaded with her to stay on, Mithila had returned to Goa with her father the very next day.

Gradually, the feelings of guilt had dissipated. Kishor had graduated as an engineer and gone off to America. Even otherwise, her crush had quickly died out. But the magic of that moment had remained firmly rooted in her mind. Sometimes when she was alone, or in her dreams, she would remember it and then she would run her tongue over her lips. She would then softly bite her lower lip and gently suck it... She would relish that moment with the anticipation that when she was married, she would once again experience that heavenly thrill.

But it didn't happen that way in real life. Kissing did not find a place in Rajesh's concept of romance. A year of marriage went by and other than planting kisses on her cheeks, Rajesh hadn't touched his lips to hers even once. Finally, one day Mithila herself had taken the initiative.

Rajesh had returned from Bombay that day. He was elated at having been selected after an interview for the post of Chief Engineer by a German company operating in Saudi Arabia. That night they had had a celebration. Knowing from past experience that Rajesh would be very aroused when happy, Mithila touched her lips to his cheek when she was in his arms. Gently turning his head, she tenderly touched her lips to his. When Rajesh tried to turn away, she firmly held his face with both hands and took his lower lip between hers. Struggling to free himself,

Rajesh had pushed her away. 'Sh-i-i! What are you doing, Mithu?'

Mithila was disappointed, but it certainly wasn't in her character to let go.

'What's wrong with you? Can't you kiss me? C'mon, give me a kiss! Please?'

Deciding to humour her, Rajesh planted a loud smack on her cheek. 'Happy now? I can't stand that lip-to-lip business!'

'But why? Try it at least…'

'No, sweetheart. I feel repelled just by the thought of the saliva…' said Rajesh, wrinkling his nose in disgust. By now Mithila had lost her ardour.

'You're crazy! When you come close together in love, it is no longer saliva. It's like an elixir…'

Rajesh interrupted her, 'How would *you* know? As if you've kissed before!'

Mithila remained silent. There was no hint of suspicion in Rajesh's question. His tone seemed to be merely saying, 'Since you've never kissed, how would you know?'

Realizing that were she to persist with the argument, Rajesh might get suspicious, Mithila had conceded the point to Rajesh.

Rajesh had initially come to Riyadh alone. Mithila had joined him three months later.

Mithila had enjoyed great happiness in the company of Rajesh. It wasn't as if they never had any tiffs, but they enjoyed a close relationship. So much so that when she'd gone home for her confinement, she'd returned to Riyadh within three months along with the newborn Babu, because she was worried about Rajesh managing alone.

The only occasional irritants were the restrictions imposed in Riyadh. One couldn't get out of the house without wearing a burqa. There was no holiday except Juma. No woman could move about unaccompanied. Even when walking with her husband, a woman had to walk one step behind him. In the parks, the men were confined to their area while the women occupied theirs. In schools, too, boys were segregated from girls—this happened even in the Montessori schools for very young children. In the kindergarten that Babu attended, though, boys and girls sat together. Next year, when he would go to the first standard, Babu would have to go to a boys-only school. Mithila made a mental note that Rajesh would have to be reminded to make arrangements for Babu's admission to the Indian School.

Wondering why Babu had still not returned, Mithila glanced up at the clock when she heard the familiar three toots of Rajesh's car. Mithila hurried to the door but waited to open it. Newly arrived in Saudi, that was the first lesson taught to her. She'd been waiting for Rajesh with the door open. Rajesh had entered and, immediately afterwards, the bell had rung. The Muthawa had ordered Rajesh in no uncertain terms to tell his wife that waiting to welcome her husband or saying goodbye to him from an open door was against the rules and if she made the mistake again, action would be taken.

When she heard Rajesh's footsteps approach, Mithila opened the door without waiting to hear the bell.

'Why did you get delayed?'

'I got held up. First there was an accident just as I was getting out of the office. I had a hard time manoeuvring my way out of that. And then, as luck would have it, I got a red signal at every cross-road, losing two minutes each time.'

'He fell asleep today, too!' Mithila commented, taking Babu from Rajesh.

'Any e-mail from Germany?'

'Nothing. I think I better give up hope,' Rajesh said, unlacing his shoes.

'Why don't you send them a message?'

'No, Mithu. It's not proper etiquette.'

'Etiquette or netiquette?' Mithila was showing off the vocabulary she'd picked up from Rajesh.

'Forget it. C'mon, let's eat quickly. I have to go back to the site. I may get delayed, so don't get worried.' And Rajesh got up. Mithila laid the sleeping Babu on the bed and served Rajesh his lunch.

As soon as Rajesh went off, she woke Babu up, took his clothes off, and gave him a bath. By the time she fed him, and had her own lunch, it was almost two-thirty.

'What did you learn in school today, Babu?' Mithila asked, opening his satchel. She found a colouring book there. It wasn't Babu's.

'Where did you get this book? Did the teacher give it to you?'

'Na go, Mummy. That's Nasleen's. She gave me!' he lisped the name. Mithila noted that he addressed her with the familiar *go* rather than the respectful *ge*, probably imitating Rajesh. Mercifully he doesn't call me Mithu, she thought wryly.

'Babu, you should not bring home other people's things, okay?'

'But I didn't take it. She gave!'

'Even if somebody gives you anything, say, "No, thank you," and give it back. What do you have to say?'

'No thanku!' Babu pronounced and, feeling pleased, clapped for himself.

'And what is this, Babu?' asked Mithila, fishing out a paper.

'Teacher gave that. She said to give it to Papa and Mummy.'

She opened it to find a note from the principal.

Dear Parents,
We request you both to come to the school office without fail at noon tomorrow with your child. We wish to discuss your child's misbehaviour with you.
Sd/
Principal

Mithila was astonished by the tone of the letter.

'Babu, what did you do in school today?'

'I did my ay-bi-shi.'

'What else did you do? You had a fight with somebody?'

'No, Mummy.'

'Did you talk back to Teacher?'

'No, Mummy. But Teacher simply scolded me.'

'But why? What did you do?'

'You know Mummy, something fell in Nasleen's eye, so I did "phoo" to blow it away.'

'Then what happened?'

'Teacher told me sit far away.'

Mithila decided that rather than questioning Babu further, it would be better to find out from the teacher tomorrow.

Normally Mithila killed time by watching TV. But today, she didn't feel like doing so. Hoping that Rajesh would come home soon, Mithila waited. But today of all days, Rajesh came later than usual. And he was in a foul mood.

'Damn these Surta!'

'What happened, Rajesh?' Mithila asked.

'On my way to the site, I got a ticket for changing lanes on the highway without signalling. I told him that my side-lights were on, but he claimed that I'd signalled late.'

'Then?'

'What else? Can we argue with them in their country? I got a challan for five hundred rials.'

'Did you pay the fine?'

'No. I have to pay it tomorrow. Which means that I'll have to go to office late.'

Five hundred rials is a small fortune—over five thousand rupees. One comes to these unfriendly places only to make money and it was but natural for Rajesh to be irritated for losing money in this way.

Mithila, who had been anxiously waiting to relieve her own tension by telling Rajesh about the letter, waited for him to wash up and then sit with the newspaper. Once he was done, she showed him the letter. Rajesh's brow wrinkled worriedly as he read it.

'Yesterday it was the Muthawa, today the Surta. I wonder what tomorrow has in store for us?' remarked Rajesh as he got up to eat.

Four-and-a-half-year-old Babu was alleged to have misbehaved. What could he have done? But there was no way of finding out—there certainly was no point in asking Babu. He must have done something innocently, but what could it be?

The next morning, Rajesh called his office to ask for half a day's leave. He first paid his traffic fine. He came back quite happy. 'One good thing is that they haven't made any endorsement on my licence. Otherwise it would have been a permanent blot.'

'Good! At least the day seems to have begun well!' remarked Mithila hopefully.

Approaching noon, even the seconds hand of the wall clock seemed to be moving lethargically.

Before noon, all three of them were at the school. On the dot at twelve, the principal called them into his office. An Arab gentleman wearing the traditional dress was already present. The principal, without bothering with a preamble, addressed them in English.

'We have received a serious complaint about your son's misconduct.'

Rajesh and Mithila were distressed, and nervous. Putting on a brave front, Rajesh asked, 'What has he done, Sir?'

With a momentary glance in the Arab's direction, the principal cleared his throat and, in a serious voice, intoned, 'Your son has kissed Mr Shabud'din's daughter, Nasreen.'

Rajesh stared incredulously. Four-and-a-half-year-old Babu had kissed Nasreen! Meaning: he had just playfully pecked her. Just that? He'd been scared that Babu had struck somebody or that he'd injured someone—even though in play—and drawn blood, or something like that. Just a kiss! But then this country was such. They probably wouldn't hesitate to lock up Babu for his sin. Or maybe even repatriate his parents!

But Mithila was not troubled about it at all. She felt elated, as if a great burden had been lifted off her head. Her face had started brightening into a smile. To hide it, she imperceptibly lowered the veil over her face. Taking hold of Babu's hand—who, all this while, had been innocently looking on—Mithila gently pressed it. Even though he was Rajesh's son, he had publicly kissed Nasreen! And without bothering about anyone, too!

'We can expel your child for this act,' the principal sternly informed them. 'But this being the first time, we are only issuing this warning. Please instruct him that if he misbehaves again, we will not tolerate it.'

Rajesh was relieved. 'I assure you of that, Sir. Thank you, Sir!' Turning towards the Arab, he apologized to him, too.

Sorry, my foot! Mithila was furious with Rajesh. While she felt like hugging Babu and patting him on the back, here was Rajesh apologizing to those men!

With the feeling that they had escaped lightly, Rajesh went out with Mithila and Babu. Normally, Babu sat in the back but, today, Mithila sat with him on the front seat.

Before starting the car, Rajesh asked, 'Babu, so you kissed Nasreen?'

'Yes, Papa. But Nasleen kissed me first!' Babu replied ingenuously.

Before Rajesh could open his mouth to say something like, 'You shouldn't do that' or 'Next time don't do such a thing', Mithila hugged Babu and asked him. 'Did you find the kiss sweet, Babu?'

Babu nodded bashfully.

'That's my boy!' Mithila squeezed him tight.

'Enough of that, Mithu! As if you have to praise him!' Rajesh remarked, starting the car. 'We were fortunate to have escaped with a warning. If he does it again…'

'So what if he does it again? At the most, they will tell us to take him away from the school. In any case, he will finish with this school in three months. We can admit him to the Indian School straightaway.'

'Instead of giving him good advice, you are doing just the opposite!' Rajesh remarked, accelerating.

'Rajesh, sometimes elders have lessons to learn from the mouths of babes!' Mithila pronounced philosophically. It could be that Rajesh did not hear Mithila over the noise of the traffic; perhaps he did not want to join the argument. The car kept moving forward.

By the time they reached home, Babu was fast asleep, as usual. Before they could unlatch the door, they could hear the phone ringing inside. Rajesh rushed in and picked up the receiver while Mithila carried Babu to the bedroom. She'd just laid Babu on the bed and had removed his shoes when Rajesh came running into the room. Happiness was writ large on his face. He pulled Mithila by the hand and hugged her. He lifted her and, twirling her around, said radiantly, 'Wonderful news, sweetheart! I've got the fellowship! Now we can all go to Germany!'

Mithila, too, became excited. Happiness was piling on happiness. Hugging him tight, she nuzzled her face against his shoulder and said, 'Congratulations, Raj!'

Rajesh's arms enveloped Mithila.

'Tighter, Raj!' Mithila's whisper fell upon his ears. Their cheeks touched. Their breaths mingled. And, almost reflexively, their lips parted.

'My Raj!' Mithila murmured as her lips touched his cheek. Rajesh too, touched his lips to Mithila's cheek. The lips slid down and touched each other. Mithila sucked his lip and involuntarily, Rajesh gripped Mithila's lip with his own. Both tongues probed each other...what a wonderful new experience! A thrilling feeling never before known.

'Mummy!'

Babu had woken up and was gaping at them wide-eyed. They both stepped apart hastily.

'Mummy, what are you doing?'

'Eh? Nothing, darling. Something fell into Papa's eye, so I made "phoo" to blow it away.'

'Papa, did you kiss Mummy?'

Rajesh, momentarily stumped at being caught in the act, laughed. 'Yes! But Mummy kissed me first!'

Mithila laughed contentedly.

In the Land of Humans

Nothing untoward had happened till they reached Ramnagar. All the bulls were walking in a straight line. At times, they would break into a trot. Halsid'du cantered along to the beat of the tinkling bells around Bud'du's neck.

Just one more day and then…Goa. He should make at least forty rupees on each bullock. Once the cattle were handed over to the butcher, all he had to do was to count the money and buy things for the return journey.

The fabled greenery of Goa, as it had been described by others to Halsid'du, appeared before his eyes and Halsid'du tingled with excitement as he lightly drew the switch over Bud'du's back. Bud'du was startled, and bolted. When he leaped, his head hit the rump of the bull in front of him. The startled bull broke away from the line and ran, tail in the air. A truck, driving behind the herd, hit the bolting bull. Bellowing in agony, the animal sprawled on the road. The truck went on its way without even pausing.

Halsid'du was terrified. What was he to do now? Quickly rounding up the other bulls, he guided them off the road into a meadow below and went back on the road.

The stricken bull turned to Halsid'du with a piteous look in its eyes. The forelegs moved, and showed that he was still alive; a rear leg was broken. Halsid'du squatted on the road by the bull's side.

Passers-by would stop for a while to look and commiserate before moving on. A truck driver paused to shower bad words on Halsid'du and then shouted, 'Move him to the side. Can't you see that he is hindering traffic?'

Whilst leaving the house, his father had given him some valuable advice. The butcher's man, too, had added some suggestions. But neither had told him what to do in case of an accident on the road.

With help from people passing by, he struggled and dragged the bull to the edge of the road. Though the bull was obviously malnourished, judging from his starkly defined ribs, it took three people to move him. Halsid'du avoided meeting the agonized eyes of the bull all along, and kept looking around desperately. In the distance, he could see a hut. Nudging the other cattle into a corner where they would not stray on to the road, Halsid'du walked to the house. An old man was sitting outside. Halsid'du asked for water. He'd asked water for the bull, but the old man brought it in a tumbler. He drank the water and told him about the injured bull. The man then filled water in a plastic bowl and gave it to Halsid'du.

Halsid'du poured the water down the bull's mouth. But he couldn't be sure how much of it the animal drank as much of it drained to the ground.

'Are you taking the bulls to Goa?' the old man asked, approaching.

Halsid'du nodded.

'Who's the agent?'

'Kassim.'

'What are you going to do now?'

Halsid'du kept silent.

'Listen to me. This bull won't be able to stand up on its feet anymore. You might as well sell him to a butcher now. You'll get something for him at least. Karim's house is just half an hour from here. Shall I call him?'

Once again Halsid'du remained quiet. The bull was resting his head on the ground. But even from that position, he continued to look towards Halsid'du with beseeching eyes. Maybe he was pleading with the cattle-driver to put an end to its agony.

'I know Kassim well. Earlier, I too used to drive cattle. My khatal was Nabi. Kassim served his apprenticeship with this Nabi. I would invariably meet him whenever I went to Goa. Now I'm too old to do these cattle drives.'

Halsid'du was engrossed in his own thoughts.

'Appa! What shall I tell the butcher? He'll....'

'Tell Kassim that Ashrumiya who lives near the dargah told you. He passes regularly this way. I, too, can inform him.'

Karim arrived with a small auto-rickshaw and squeezed the big bull into it.

'It will be an agony for him. He will get hurt.'

Seeing Halsid'du cringe, Karim smirked. 'He's not being taken to be reared. He's off to slaughter.'

Karim was about to leave when Halsid'du softly asked the old man, 'The money?'

'If you ask him for money, he'll take it for a song. I've told him to settle with Kassim. This is the normal route for Kassim. He, too, knows him. Tell Kassim that I said this to you.'

Halsid'du was relieved.

Halsid'du had to spend the night there. He soaked some oilcake in a vessel he had borrowed from Ashrumiya. Then, as if he was distributing precious prasad to Goddess Yellamma, he took the feed and gave each bull a little. Thereafter, he poured water into the vessel, stirred it, and gave it to the animals to drink. He then rounded them in a circle with Bud'du, who was mooing softly, in the middle.

Amma had given him food packed in a cloth bag. Halsid'du had used Bud'du's horns as a peg to suspend the bag. Halsid'du now removed the bag and, using the same vessel which he'd given to the bulls to drink out of, got some water for himself. He spread his things under a nearby tree. He must have been very hungry. He downed three thick chapatis of jowar, dipping them in garlic chutney. He craved more but, clamping down on his still unsatiated hunger, he tied up his lunch pack. He still had half the bhakris left in the pack, but he needed to save them for the return trip. He drank some water and, after belching expansively, lay down in the shade of the tree.

There was a similar tree in front of his house, slightly bigger than this one. Last winter, all the leaves had fallen off and now, even ten months later, the new leaves were yet to sprout. But then, what else can one expect when the rains were so delayed? He had a thousand questions but he had given up. But this tree had beautiful leaves. And, in Goa, it seemed as if everything was so green!

'When you're grown up, go to Goa and live like a man.' This had been Appu's advice to Halsid'du. To do the things that he himself wanted to, but could not.

His village, seven miles in the interior of Khanapur, did not have a single school.

Appu's father had heard one of Babasaheb Ambedkar's speeches. So he'd told Appu, 'Get an education and be a man.'

Appu had gone to school and got a primary education. But he hadn't come up in life. Later, many children from Mharvaddo, the ghetto where the scheduled castes of the village lived, went to school. Some even reached high school. But those that remained behind in the village did not come up in life. Those who went to Khanapur and Belgaum did better for themselves than those who stayed back. But Appu had seen a better world elsewhere. Some of his acquaintances had migrated to Goa and Appu had visited them a few times. Having seen the lives they led there, Appu had advised Halsid'du, 'It doesn't matter if you don't get much of an education, but see that when you're grown up, you go to Goa. You'll live like a human being there.'

Halsid'du had grown up dreaming of living in Goa like a man. But, there were no signs yet that this dream would materialize.

It was when the khatal, the cattle-brokers, reached the village that Halsid'du's hopes received a boost. There was a drought in the region. The bellies of the farmers were hollowed out by hunger and their stomachs were now touching their backbones. Even in the homes of those who were better off, the fires were lit just once to cook the sole meal of the day. If this was the state humans lived in, could they even think of the animals? Forget about the older animals, one could count the ribs even on the young bulls. To add to their misery, they'd been yoked to the plough in vain anticipation of the rains. This had caused bloody sores on their necks where the yoke had rasped the skin. Who would want these oxen with oozing necks? Cattle, which had been nurtured like one's own children, had now become a burden to the farmers. This sorry state of affairs was the happy hunting ground for the khatals who would buy cattle from these distressed farmers for a song and make a killing by selling them to distant butchers.

Sporting a pagree on his head, the bearded Kassim had ridden from Goa into the village. He first assessed the need of the desperate farmers and then made his offers. The poor farmers gratefully accepted what he was giving them without bothering to bargain.

Halsid'du, too, had a bull, and he did not want to part with him. But he knew that Appu wouldn't allow him to keep it. But surprise of surprises, Appu himself announced that he was not selling it. The broker needed a cattle-driver to take the cattle to Goa. Appu had already gauged this need when Kassim had reached the village. 'This is Halsid'dappa. He is tough and wiry. He'll make a good cattle-driver.'

There were several candidates for the job, but the broker chose Halsid'du after gauging his strength, capability and enthusiasm. Only then did his father reveal his plans to Halsid'du. Instead of selling Bud'du to the broker, Halsid'du could take him to Goa along with the twelve others that Kassim had bought. After handing over Kassim's twelve, he could sell Bud'du for a better price in Goa. Halsid'du was greatly impressed by Appu's brains.

The broker had brought medical certificates from the vet for only the twelve, but Appu reasoned, 'What difference will it make, who bothers to count?'

The formalities of getting the bulls shoed for the journey at the blacksmith's, painting their horns green to distinguish them, and getting certificates from the veterinarian was all handled by the broker's man. Before handing over their cattle, the villagers had removed the bells from their necks. But Halsid'du had not removed the one hanging from Bud'du's neck, deciding that he would do so just before selling him.

Amma had baked a lot of jowar bhakris for Halsid'du, and had packed appetizing garlic chutney along with them. As she cooked she went on prattling, 'The feast of Goddess Saundatti Yellamma is fast approaching. We have to spend five nights there. You'll have to come back from Goa as soon as your work is done. We'll take Anshi along with us to Yellamma's feet. Don't delay your return. If you manage to make good money on this trip we can have your wedding soon after the feast and bring Anshi into the family.'

Halsid'du was glad that Appu and Amma had eventually
approved of his choice: Anshi. Last year, just before the
feast of Yellamma, he had seen the girl flattening out cow-
dung cakes for fuel in the neighbouring ward where the
Maangas lived. She had her ghagra tucked between her
legs and her youthfulness was bursting out of her tattered
blouse. Her tousled hair was dangling over her eyes.
Suddenly, conscious of Halsid'du's stare, she became ill at
ease. As she brushed the hair from her eyes with dung-
smeared hands, some of the stuff had stuck to her cheek.
Seeing this, Halsid'du had laughed. She'd blushed in
confusion. The next time he saw her was when they were
camped on the hillock for the feast of Yellamma. Initially
bashful, they had merely exchanged glances. On the last
night of the zatra, Halsid'du had pulled her into the bushes,
hugged her tight, and whispered, 'You tell your mother. I,
too, will tell my parents.'

But when he told his parents, his father had reacted
sharply, 'How can this be? They are Maangas, and we are
Mahars!' Amma had elaborated. 'Maangas rank lower than
us. But they consider themselves superior.'

Halsid'du went for the jugular. 'Is this what Babasaheb
Ambedkar taught us?' That put an end to it, and the
proposal went through. Now all that was needed was for
him to make some money.

When the truck hit the bull, Halsid'du was afraid that
he would now have to compensate the broker. Thank
God for Ashrumiya. That Ashrumiya, who lives next to
the dargah. So there is a dargah here. First thing in the

morning, I must visit it. Whoever be the pir there, I'll pray to him for my early marriage. I'll vow to bring Anshi to the feet of this saint.

After that memorable evening when he'd held Anshi tight in his arms, he did what he did every night thereafter—he turned to his side, folded both legs inward to his belly, put both his hands between his thighs and, amid heavy breathing, drifted off to sleep.

The moon was still shining when he woke up. He went to the dargah and prayed silently standing outside. As he roused the squatting bulls, the smell of dung and urine wafted into his nostrils. Idly thinking that all this dung would have sufficed for at least two dozen cakes, he started driving the cattle even before daybreak.

The vegetation turned greener the closer they came to Goa. The bulls quickened their gait as if they, too, were longing to reach their destination. At every narrow bend in the road, Halsid'du took care to hustle the bulls to the side. Despite all this caution, some truck drivers would slow down needlessly to scream abuses at him. By noon, the road had heated up. Halsid'du removed the sandals Appu had given him from the horns of Bud'du where he'd hung them and put them on. Neither he nor the animals were used to walking on the tarmac road. Shoes had been hammered on to the hooves of the bulls for this. Halsid'du had no sandals. This was the only pair that Appu possessed—that, too, made of pure leather, which he'd walked off with from the heap outside a temple. Though he hardly ever wore the sandals, he regularly cleaned and oiled them and flaunted the pair maybe once a year. He wouldn't even dream of allowing Halsid'du to wear them, but this time, he himself had given them to Halsid'du. saying, 'Wear them only when the road feels hot.' After walking for an hour, though, the sandals began to bite. His attention began to stray from the bulls onto his footwear. Finally, he removed the sandals and put them back in the plastic bag and hung it back on the bull's horn.

At the Karnataka border post, the papers were perfunctorily checked, 'Kassim's bulls? Twelve, right? Okay go.' At the Goa checkpost, the cattle were vaccinated and meticulously counted. Kassim had obviously tipped them for twelve animals. Had there been thirteen, Halsid'du might have been in trouble. Since one bull had died, there was no problem for Bud'du to go through.

Thank God! I've reached Goa at last. I must look out for work here. I must look for a place to stay. I have to become a man, thought Halsid'du. Appu had told him to not come back with just the money. Instead, he told him to invest in some bottles of liquor. 'Liquor is cheap in Goa. We'll get double the money if we sell it in Khanapur.' Appu's business sense has to be admired, but I'll spend some money on things for Amma and Appu and Anshi, too.

He was to meet Kassim at Tiska junction which, he was told, was at the end of a march four hours long from the border. It will be midnight by the time I reach. I had better camp here for the night. Selecting an open space by the side of the road, Halsid'du once again made the bulls squat in a circle around Bud'du, opened his tiffin and had his supper. Drawing up his knees, he went to sleep, once again dreaming of Anshi like the night before.

Even before dawn, the bells around Bud'du's neck began tinkling to the beat of his hooves, anxious to resume the journey. The lush green vegetation all around was punctuated with abundant water besides countless public taps reassured Halsid'du. Anshi will not have to toil here. The people here were good too, he'd been told. He should stay here in Goa with Anshi and live like a real human being.

A meeting was in progress near a temple along the road. A man wearing a long kurta was making a loud speech, and was being frequently applauded by the gathering. Halsid'du slowed down. The sun had started to dazzle his eyes. Hunger was gnawing at him. Should he take a break and eat the bhakri here or should he have it after reaching his destination? He wondered idly about the meeting. Was it an election meeting?

'Love animals. Do not treat them cruelly. Stop those who ill-treat animals! The law is on your side! Report the poachers! Can we deny animals their right to live only to satisfy our gluttony? Stop animal sacrifices! God needs neither chickens nor goats to be sacrificed to him! The slaughter of cattle should be banned...'

Somebody from the audience shouted, 'Look! There on the road! Those cattle are being taken to be slaughtered!'

Halsid'du wouldn't have been amused had he known why all the people turned to look in his direction.

Deriving strength from the intervention, the speaker thundered into the mike, 'See for yourselves. Do we revere the cow as our mother and Nandi the bull as the vehicle of God Shiva or do we not? We can eat only because these cattle plough our fields! Are we then, going to fold our arms and watch mutely as these cattle are being taken to be butchered?'

Halsid'du could not follow the language being spoken by the gathering. Soon, the crowd from the meeting took off like an incensed mob. As he was wondering where they were headed, they reached the main road and, picking up whatever stones and sticks that they could find, they rushed towards him. Shouting and gesticulating, they began to scatter and chase away the bulls. When Bud'du, too, joined in the stampede, Halsid'du jumped in to restrain him. The mob caught hold of Halsid'du and, after chasing away Bud'du, they began to hammer him even as he vainly tried to retrieve the tiffin bag that had fallen off Bud'du's horns.

'You want to take cattle for slaughter, eh? You people need to be taught a lesson! Take this!' said a man as he slapped Halsid'du hard across the face.

'Gai bailon ki qatl karni hai? See how this hurts,' said another man as he landed a kick on Halsid'du and, then, like a swarm of enraged bees, the mob set upon him.

The great lovers of animals pounded Halsid'du to their hearts' content.

At the end of it all, Halsid'du was left wondering why he had been beaten black and blue by those who lived in this land of humans.

Misconceptions

'Oh my! Have you seen this? Damn these rats!' Sulbha was in tears.

'You are cursing these rats every day now. What have they destroyed today?'

'Look at this saree. They've chewed the pallu to bits!'

Ratnakar looked up. The border of Sulbha's new saree had indeed been gnawed at by rats. And such an expensive saree, too—a gorgeous Kanjeevaram!

'Where did you keep it? You should have kept it in a safe place!' Ratnakar was irritated. He would have scolded her even more, but her teary eyes restrained him.

'Just the day before yesterday, I had removed it and kept it on the line... My beautiful new...'

'Forget it. Wear another one now.'

'I'll have to wear another one, of course. But this one...'

'Didn't I bring home a nice new rat-trap? You wouldn't leave me alone till I brought it.' The money Ratnakar had paid for the saree danced before his eyes. It had been a big chunk of his salary!

'Buying a trap is not enough. Don't you have to bait and set it?' Sulbha remarked as she unfolded another saree.

'If you couldn't do it, you should have told me!' retorted Ratnakar. But he immediately remembered. The night before, Sulbha had told him to bait the trap, but he had been tired and sleepy, and had neglected to do it. Before Sulbha could bring it up, he said, 'Forget it now. Tonight, remind me before we go to bed... Once I'm in bed, I feel reluctant to get up.'

'These wretched rats have become bolder than ever since the cat died,' Sulbha grumbled as she draped her saree. 'And what prolific breeders—a bushel of babies in each litter!'

Sulbha's anger had taken off in a different direction.

'Don't worry, Sulbha. You, too, will have babies...'

After Ratnakar's tender words, Sulbha calmed down. She turned and looked into his eyes and read both encouragement and support in them. She came close to Ratnakar and put her head on his chest. She then silently moved away and, with renewed interest, stood before the mirror.

Today, they had planned to visit the temple. Ratnakar, though a believer, was not an ardent devotee. He didn't like to approach God for every minor thing. But today he was compelled to go. Last week, his elder sister had said to him—that, too, in front of Sulbha. 'Look here, Ratnu, hear me out. Uday, who got married around the time you did, already has two kids. Chandrakant's wife is expecting their second. I kept silent all this time thinking that you might have been planning or something. I have decided to speak out now. Mother and Father had an abiding faith in our family god. I, too, have great faith in Him. Go to the temple and petition Him with prasad. Don't say no to me. Listen to your elder sister. There just might be some unfulfilled vow or something...'

Ratnakar took this with a smile. For him prasad was just a superstition. But Sulbha was insistent. And, believing that there was no harm in trying, he'd agreed to go. They were supposed to have gone the previous Sunday itself, but couldn't, since Sulbha was having her period then. They'd both looked forward to the visit today but Sulbha had discovered, as soon as they woke up, the rat-gnawed saree. Ever since their cat had died, the rats had multiplied. Moreover, the cat had died after they had given its kittens away. Had it died earlier, they could have kept one from the litter. With no cat in the house, the rats had grown very bold. Nothing escaped their attention. You couldn't help but admire the way they tackled onions and potatoes—leaving the outer skin intact, they would hollow out the core! Bananas and apples were, of course, their staple. Once they'd even removed the cigarettes from a packet that had been left on the table and chewed them up. Who would believe it!

One morning, Sulbha had told him, 'Today, the rats ate all the biscuits from the tin.' Ratnakar had scolded her, 'You're so careless! Why did you leave the tin open?'

Sulbha had replied, 'But I didn't! It was they who did it.'

Ratnakar had ridiculed her. But, later, he realized that she could have been right. So he had bought a rat-trap and, after baiting it, set it out. The morning after, hearing Sulbha vomiting, Ratnakar, who was normally a late riser, had jumped out of bed. Thinking that it was morning sickness, Ratnakar ran to her in excitement only to find that a young rat had been caught between the teeth of the trap he'd set the night before, and its entrails had spilled out. Even Ratnakar had felt his gorge rise at the sight.

This was the first and last rat caught in that trap. Somebody explained that once a rat gets caught in a trap, others shy away from the odour of the blood. So Ratnakar had bought a different kind of trap only yesterday. This was constructed in the form of a cage whose trap-door would snap shut after the rat had entered it. This would be good! One rat every night! Remove the live rat in the morning, dispose of him, and set the trap again the next evening. There would be no odour of blood or of the dead rat. A rat a day...thirty a month...and in a year...

'I'm ready! Only, you're not. Don't blame me if we miss the bus.'

Ratnakar dressed quickly and the two set out.

Sulbha was happy. She liked going to the temple and attending religious ceremonies there. But today she had a special reason, a special request to God. 'Listen, Ratnakar, today you must pray from the bottom of your heart, okay?'

Ratnakar was sceptical but he didn't want to hurt Sulbha. So he smiled and said, 'Sure, I will.'

'Let's hope that we face no problems; let's hope that our forebears have left no vows unfulfilled...'

He felt like saying, 'The only problem we have is these rats. Besides them, there's no other problem.' But he didn't want to dissipate the warm, expectant glow on Sulbha's face. He looked at Sulbha. She looked so beautiful today!

There were other people at the temple waiting for prasad. Standing in queue, waiting for his turn, Ratnakar was bored. Each devotee had his own problems. For some, the paklli, the ritual in which the priest let offered petals drop from the statue of the deity and then interpreted them, was quick. Others had to wait for almost an hour. Some wanted prasad to get engaged or married. Others sought divine opinion on buying a car. Taking prasad from one petitioner, the priest would plead with God; with some other petitioner, the priest might admonish Him.

Had he known that he would have to wait for so long, Ratnakar would never have come. He would have gone back even now, but for Sulbha. She wasn't bored. Having already completed a series of fervent perambulations round the sanctum sanctorum, and a few around the temple itself, she now sat motionless with her eyes fixed on the deity. Looking at Sulbha's radiant face, Ratnakar was reminded of the picture of Mirabai, the poet-saint who was a great devotee of Lord Krishna. Humbled by Sulbha's great faith in God, Ratnakar felt that he, too, should join her in prayer. Momentarily, he joined his hands.

The priest motioned to them. 'Okay, now you two may come forward.'

After asking their names and from where they had come, the priest invoked the deity's blessings on them. He then got down to business. 'What is your problem?' Hearing the priest's query, Ratnakar fumbled for a moment. Sulbha giggled softly, and gave him a 'You tell' look.

'I…we…have been married almost…no, completed three years…'

'Go on!' The priest was in a hurry.

'We…in our home…there is still no…'

'You still do not have children, is that so?' the priest interrupted.

Ratnakar nodded and glanced around furtively. But, after a gentle pinch from Sulbha, he focused his eyes on the deity in front. The priest asked for a petal. He then uttered a loud incantation to the deity. Two minutes went by, three minutes. Five minutes had passed. Ratnakar began to feel restless. Sulbha, with a calm mind, gazed at the deity with great concentration.

As soon as one of the several petals dropped, the priest looked at Ratnakar.

Ratnakar looked up anxiously.

'The God is angry!' the priest pronounced, as if he himself were angry.

'Why?'

'Perhaps you have committed some transgression.'

Ratnakar and Sulbha both stared at one another.

'Try and recall. Clarify it, here and now,' the priest advised sternly.

'What transgression?' Ratnakar asked in astonishment.

'How can I know that? I only know that it has been recorded in His court,' said the priest, like a police inspector addressing a thief.

'But we do not recall anything,' Ratnakar said, looking towards Sulbha, who nodded at him.

'In that case, we have to ask God to help you remember what the sin of commission or omission is,' said the priest.

'What could the sin of commission or omission be?' Sulbha asked the priest.

'It could be an unfulfilled vow, or a lack of offerings for the souls of your ancestors, or maybe you have neglected to offer the tribute of liquor and bread to the Evil One. When there is a defilement or maybe an injury caused to the cobra-guardian of your environs, this particular petal could also drop,' the priest had explained in plain words, but he was pressed for time. 'Let it be for now. You don't remember, right? I shall ask God to remind you.' And he began his loud peroration:

'Lord God, it is true that Thou art angered! But have mercy on Thy children who have come to Thy feet with great faith. They do not recall the nature of their sin. Therefore, in Thy great mercy, help them to remember, maybe when they are awake or in their dreams, maybe right now or maybe later. Meanwhile give them Thy assurance that their wishes will be fulfilled.'

Another few minutes went by. Ratnakar and Sulbha were lost in thought. Could they have forgotten a coconut that they had dedicated to God? Could they have broken a tradition or neglected a ritual? As they thought along these lines, the petals dropped. With a smile, the priest picked it up. He said a final prayer for their protection and assured them, 'Your wishes will be fulfilled. But, meanwhile, if you do remember or get a hint about the problem, do not fail to come here.'

With that he tucked the petals into their hands and wished them goodbye.

They had lunch at a relative's house in Ponda and returned home in the evening. Ratnakar was relieved. He felt that the prasad had gone off rather well. And since the responsibility of reminding them about the sins or transgressions of the past was now squarely on God's shoulders, there was no need to worry about it. But Sulbha's mind was still wholly working in the past. She was quiet throughout the journey back home.

'Did you make any vow before our wedding?' she asked, all of a sudden.

'Never in my life!' Ratnakar said emphatically.

Sulbha lapsed into silence once again. As they reached home, she suddenly remembered. 'The spot where we built our bathroom, could a cobra have a burrow there? What if it was a cobra-guardian?'

'For God's sake, shut up! Don't worry unnecessarily. When we built the bathroom there, there was no cobra's burrow, not even a rat tunnel! Only now have the rats dug many tunnels.'

But even after supper, Sulbha's forehead was still creased.

'Forget it now! Hasn't the priest said that God will remind us? That's it!' Ratnakar felt sleepy. He saw the rat-gnawed saree lying on the bed. It was a good reminder, he thought, and got up. He brought the new rat-trap and, baiting it with a sliced potato, set it where the saree had been chewed up the previous night. He fell into a sound sleep.

Suddenly, Sulbha prodded him awake. 'Listen! I remember.'

'What? Remember what?' asked Ratnakar, rubbing his eyes.

'What the priest said.'

'What?'

'Don't you remember that our cat had littered last year?'

'Yes...' Ratnakar was wide awake now.

'Where did you leave the kittens?'

'At Tolleaband on the bank of the lake. Why?'

'Were there any houses close by?'

In fact, there had been no house close by, but just to get Sulbha off his back, he said, 'Yes, a little way off.'

'The kittens probably never reached there. They must have... Could they have died?'

Not knowing what to say, Ratnakar remained silent.

'It must be that! We must be suffering from their curses.' Resting her head on Ratnakar's chest, Sulbha continued in a tearful voice, 'And the poor cat died soon after too. It is that...the curses of the cat.'

'You crazy girl! The cat died of sickness, not of heartbreak at the loss of her kittens. And you are only presuming that the kittens have died. I am telling you that they have not. They must be alive somewhere.'

Ratnakar managed to pacify Sulbha, but he himself just could not go back to sleep. Those kittens that he'd abandoned had started frolicking before his eyes.

The next morning, he woke up a little late. In his haste to get to work, he just managed to see a big fat rat caught in the trap. 'Very good! Aren't you the one who gnawed the saree? I'll take care of you today!'

Since he had got up late, Ratnakar deferred the despatching of the rat for the evening and set out for work.

'Look here, I don't want that rat-trap in the house. Just keep it out in the corner. Just looking at it scares me!'

'You're really silly, my girl. Are you scared of a trapped rat?' Ratnakar admonished. But he made sure that he kept the rat-trap by the side of the bathroom outside before leaving for work.

When he returned in the evening, he found Sulbha standing in the doorway, anxiously waiting for him. Her face seemed to be glowing with excitement.

'What's up? You're looking radiant!' Ratnakar said.

'Shall I tell?'

'Spill it out.'

'The prasad has worked.'

Ratnakar was amazed. It had been barely eight days since she had her period. How could...

'What makes you say so?'

'Come, I'll show you...' Sulbha pulled Ratnakar inside.

Pointing a finger at the rat-trap, Sulbha pushed Ratnakar forward. Ratnakar saw that the rat had littered three tiny rats inside the trap! Even Ratnakar's masculine heart trembled. His throat constricted. The mother-rat eyed him in trepidation. She seemed to be pleading with him.

'Wait...' Ratnakar turned round. He seemed to be searching for something in the backyard.

'I've located it...' Sulbha told him.

'What?'

'This!' Sulbha indicated a rat-hole.

Ratnakar gently lifted the rat-trap. He took it to the mouth of the burrow and lifted the trap-door. The rat skipped into the tunnel. Ratnakar then carefully lowered the little pink rats into the tunnel. And, without looking back, they returned to the house.

The Cynic

I had a couple of things to do so I'd gone to Margao. Around eleven, I was at Vasudev's shop in town. There, I met Baboy.

'Where to, Baboy?' Though he was my maternal uncle, I addressed him the way everybody did.

'Can't you see? I'm right here!' Baboy enjoyed a putdown.

'That's apparent, but...'

'You know that tale of Birbal's, don't you?'

'Which one?'

'Once Emperor Akbar asked Birbal how many blind persons there were in his kingdom. So Birbal...'

'I know the story. You are reminding me of it because I asked you an obvious question.'

Baboy laughed. It was his usual habit. But I wasn't angry. People rarely get irritated with Baboy, not immediately at least.

'How's everyone at home?' I asked.

'Fine!'

'And the grandchildren?' Baboy had got his eldest son married at a young age. And now, before he'd crossed fifty-five, he was already the grandfather of two.

'Excellent!' Baboy always replied in this fashion.

Turning to Vasudev, I asked, 'Have you heard from Madhav?'

'No letter from him for over a month. We're quite worried,' replied Vasudev, his forehead creased.

'Worried because there's no letter?' Baboy interjected. 'You have cause to worry when you receive a letter. Why a letter, you say? Is someone sick? Or does someone need money? No letter simply means that nothing extraordinary has happened which merits a letter. In other words, he's fine.'

Laughing at the logic, Vasudev got back to his work. At that moment Vasudev's helper inadvertently knocked down a standing bag of sugar, spilling a pile of it on to the floor.

Vasudev became angry and vented his spleen on the helper. Anyone would feel annoyed when so much sugar was wasted. But Baboy wasn't in the least sympathetic about the loss.

'Listen, Vasudev! The Gita says: "Krodhat bhavati sammohah sammohat smriti vibhramah smritibrunshat budhinasho budhinashat vinashyati". Translated from Sanskrit it means: "Anger leads to…"'

Vasudev, already livid, cut him short. 'Enough, Baboy! I know it. Don't add fuel to fire!'

'I don't think you have understood the meaning…'

'I have!'

'One who persists in his mistakes is called a fool!' declared an unfazed Baboy with a laugh.

'Say what you like. Anyone would be angered by so much wastage!'

'You invite vinash, destruction itself. Have you ever seen me angry?' With that, Baboy silenced Vasudev.

As a matter of fact, Baboy never got angry. He knew only one thing: accept everything with a laugh. He would laugh when anything good happened and he would laugh when anything bad happened. When someone said a good word to him, he would laugh and when anyone insulted him, then, too, he would laugh.

Vasudev had been silenced but he was still fuming at his helper, who, guilt-ridden, had bent down and was carefully gathering the top layers of the spilt sugar and putting it back in the sack. But what of the sugar that had touched the floor? Vasudev ordered him to keep it apart. When he had finished, he told the boy, 'That is more than two kilos. You take it and bring the money. Had this been the first time, I would have forgiven you. But just the other day, you poured kerosene into the edible oil and lost me a lot of money. I'm warning you; bring me the money or watch out!'

I felt a little sorry for the boy, but what Vasudev said wasn't wrong either. Some time ago, the neighbour's goats used to come into our garden and destroy the plants. We tried telling him a number of times but to no avail. It was only after we impounded the goats and extracted compensation from him that the menace stopped. From then on, not a single goat has laid a hoof in our garden. It's perfectly true—nobody reforms unless punished.

I got up to go.

'Where are you going now?' Baboy asked me.

'I have some work at the bank. After that, I'll go straight home,' I said.

'Did you bring the car?'

'Yes. Once you're used to a vehicle, you can't seem to manage on foot,' I laughed wryly.

'Could we just drop in at the hospital?' Baboy rose.

'No problem.'

I started the vehicle but, just as I was shifting into second gear, Baboy called out, 'Stop, please wait a second.'

I stopped. Baboy got out of the car. 'Bhimappa!'

The ghanti helper-boy who had spilt the sugar was standing there. He hurried over.

Fishing out a currency note from his pocket, Baboy handed it over to him, saying, 'Give this to your boss. One shouldn't be indebted to anybody. Otherwise, because of a small amount, you may have double the labour extracted from you.'

After sitting in the car, he called out to him again, 'See, don't you tell him that I gave you the money!'

'See that *you* don't tell Vasudev either,' Baboy admonished me.

I finished my work at the bank and returned.

'Did you withdraw or deposit money?'

'I withdrew.'

'Very good! Withdrawing money is good. Those who deposit are fools!'

'Fools?' True, I'd withdrawn money today; but I could do that only because I'd deposited some earlier.

'Sure they're fools! We struggle, we earn, and then we take all that money and deposit it in the bank! Isn't that foolishness? The accumulation of wealth is bad. Intellectuals accumulate knowledge and dispense it and, no matter how liberally they give it away, it never diminishes. Foolish people accumulate wealth, and just so that friends, neighbours and relatives may not borrow from them, they keep the money in the hands of a complete stranger—the bank!'

It is interesting to listen to Baboy. With his vast reading and his thirst for knowledge, he is riveting whichever subject he decides to speak on. His concerns are unusual, and he is absolutely unrestrained by the conventions of society or by etiquette.

Baboy never uses soap while bathing and also advises others not to use it—you need only ask Baboy the number of diseases one can get by using soap! Baboy never takes any medicines and does not give them to others. How antibiotics destroy good bacteria along with the bad, how a number of medications cause blood pressure to shoot up—he can even convince a doctor, temporarily at least, with his arguments. If you want to know the damage that a brush and toothpaste can cause to your teeth and gums, ask Baboy. He himself uses only neem twigs or mango leaves to clean his teeth, and decrees that his entire household do the same. He sent his children to school, but he never checked to see if they were studying properly or not.

Seeing that all his children were doing badly, I asked

him one day, 'You never ever tell the children to study. You don't even scold them when they don't study. How will they manage?'

Baboy replied, 'I have admitted them to school and my obligation has ended. As the saying goes, "You may lead a horse to water, but you cannot force it to drink." If they're thirsty for knowledge, they'll study!'

'Enough of your dialectics! Are you saying that you are not bothered if your children study or not?'

'If they study, that's good! But who says it will help them? Why do we need to study? To earn money; isn't that so? How much did Bandodkar or Chowgule study? Or, for that matter, Birla?' he asked, referring to Goa's first chief minister and top local and national industrialists.

Nobody has a reply to his questions. People may not agree with what he says, but no one can refute his devastating logic. And so Baboy ends up winning all his arguments.

He knows the Ramayana and the Mahabharata thoroughly. The Bhagvadgita is at the tip of his tongue. He has digested both the Old and New Testaments of the Bible and he can discourse with authority on Allah the Beneficent and Merciful as he has studied the Koran.

Baboy, who has done his Setimo Ano do Liceu, which was the highest level of non-professional studies in Portuguese Goa, admires the writings of the Austrian-born pacifist and biographer Stefan Zweig. He respects Gorky and Tolstoy and looks up to the greatness of Lenin, Gandhi and Nehru. He's read the philosopher Rahul Sankrityayan well enough to quote him.

I've never been able to solve this riddle: How could this intelligent and well-educated man's four sons, good-looking and smart though they are, just drop out of school and remain idle at home? The eldest, Madhu, is twenty-five—Baboy got him married, when he was just twenty-two, to the young daughter of an impoverished relation because the house needed a woman. The death of Baboy's wife at childbirth, during her seventh pregnancy, had left a void in the house, which needed to be filled. Within the next three years, Baboy had two grandchildren.

Baboy's house is in Sanvordem. That is to say, his domicile. All his work revolves around Margao. No one knows what his income is yet his house never lacks rice. But, beyond that, little else comes in. The less one eats, the better one's health, is yet another of Baboy's maxims.

I was musing on this while Baboy was talking away. 'There's one thing. A half-wit is better than a madman. But not a fool. Think about it. Suppose a relation or neighbour fails to return a hundred rupees that he'd borrowed from you, it doesn't bother you much. You even don't mind the financial loss. But if somebody takes you for a ride, that hurts. The idea that someone has made a fool of you undermines your ego. Much more than the financial loss...'

'Where to now? The hospital?' I cut in.

'Yes... But there's a thing about fools. They have absolutely no concept of happiness or sorrow. You've heard the story of fools rushing in where angels fear to tread...' He prattled on.

Baboy has always ranted against medicines and hospitals. Why then...

'Why the hospital?' I asked, interrupting his inane flow of words, which was beginning to bother me.

'Madhu's little son is not too well. We've brought him for a check-up.'

'What's the problem?'

'Diarrhoea and vomiting. He hasn't retained anything since yesterday.'

'It's past twelve-thirty now! Will Madhu still be there?' I asked.

'Madhu and his wife have both come to admit the child to the hospital. If the doctor decides to discharge him, they will go to Keshav's house.' Keshav is Baboy's younger brother who lives at Gogol in Margao.

By this time, we were at the gate of the Hospicio Hospital. Madhu was standing right at the entrance. It just didn't seem possible that this youth in shorts and shirt would be the father of two!

Madhu had a vacant look about him. I called out, but he did not respond. Baboy asked him, 'What's happened?'

Damming the flow of his tears, Madhu said in a choked voice, 'He died.'

'Where's Mali?' Baboy's countenance was composed.

'I dropped her off at Gogol. I haven't told her anything.'

The pain in Madhu's face was eloquent. My heart turned to lead.

'Good! Have you collected the death certificate and the other papers?'

Madhu drew out a bunch of papers from his pocket.

'Okay! You come with me.' Baboy stepped forward briskly.

Madhu had been avoiding my gaze all along but, when his eyes finally met mine, he could restrain himself no longer and broke into sobs.

I hugged him, patted his back gently and asked him to control himself. We went inside the hospital. The nurse indicated the cot on which the little bundle lay in eternal sleep.

A one-year-old child, this, but the form was that of a three-month-old baby. Not that it was physically retarded from birth. A child who is fed regularly does not look like this. I was sobbing inwardly but, steeling myself, I controlled my own tears.

'Pick him up. Let's take him away.' Baboy's tone was calm.

With filial obedience, Madhu stepped forward. As he was lifting the tiny body, his paternal heart convulsed and tears flooded his eyes. Madhu lifted the body up with the same care and gentleness with which he had brought the boy in. With Baboy leading, and Madhu bringing up the rear, our little procession set off. We got into the car.

'Drop us off at the station. We are going to Sanvordem by the one-thirty train,' Baboy said.

'What? With him?' I asked.

'What's the problem? First we will go to Gogol and collect Madhu's wife. Then, you can take us to the station. Once we are at Sanvordem, we are on home turf. Over here, we'll have to struggle with the arrangements.'

Baboy's insensitive attitude was beginning to make me distinctly uncomfortable. Madhu sat in the back seat, hugging his child's body and weeping.

'The arrangements in the crematorium here in Margao are good, Baboy,' I said calmly, though I was seething at him.

'In that case, we'll do this. First we'll go to Babu's shop, pay the crematorium fees there, and collect the authorization papers.'

'With him?' My eyes were retreating into their sockets.

'Okay. We'll leave Madhu at Gogol and then finish whatever has to be done.'

We took Madhu to Gogol. I stopped the car at the door. I thought that Baboy would go inside and console his daughter-in-law but Baboy got out and held the door open for his son. Madhu got out, carrying his little burden.

'You go in. Tell them to light a lamp.' Having issued these brief instructions, Baboy took his seat in the car again.

How did this happen? Why did Baboy become such an insensitive being? Or was he just afraid to confront the truth?

I turned the car. We had to hurry to make the payment before Babu's shop closed for lunch.

Finding me silent, Baboy laughed.

'Do you know? Death is part of nature! It is the most natural act. It is birth which is an accident! As a matter of fact, one must grieve when somebody is born, thinking of all the trials and tribulations this new life must go through.'

I listened dumbly.

'And crying over dead people is sheer madness! What dies is the body; the soul is immortal! What we grieve for is the body, isn't it? And what is the body? Mud! As long as there is life in it, it is human; a lifeless body is mud!'

I could see Madhu's grief-stricken face in front of my eyes, as well as that of the mother's. My own two children flashed before my eyes. I felt another wrench in my stomach.

'We give affection and love to the body, the physical form. We must learn to love the soul, the spiritual self...'

Baboy's words bounced off my ears. I felt like asking him, 'We should grieve at birth and, at death, we should set off firecrackers of joy for having broken out of the evil cycle of life. Is that it?' but the words did not come.

We arrived just as they were shutting shop. I entered and asked them to prepare the receipt which would have to be shown at the crematorium. Since the child had not yet completed a year, and had not sprouted any teeth, he could only be buried. As the receipt was being written out, I glanced outside. Somebody hailed Baboy. 'Hi there, Baboy! Where are you going?'

'Nowhere. I'd come here for some little work.'

I took out my purse to pay the fee of two rupees but—

'No, please don't.' Baboy stopped me, and insisted on paying the amount himself.

Buying a yard of white lawn cloth, we made our way to the crematorium.

'It's a good thing we decided to have it here! I'm sort of

drawn to this crematorium. Our forefathers and relations, they are all here, aren't they?'

I've been to the crematorium a number of times. I've heard two traders at a funeral talking business. I've seen people gossiping about their neighbours. Why, I myself have talked about worldly matters. But at the funerals of outsiders. From the detached way that Baboy was speaking, it would seem that it was the funeral of some distant neighbour's child that was underway.

Parking the car at the door of the crematorium, we went inside. The attendant had gone out for lunch and would be back soon.

I'd wanted to ask Baboy a question for quite some time and so I went ahead now.

'Tell me one thing, Baboy! When you brought the child to the hospital, did you know how bad he was?'

'Yes. The doctor from Sanvordem sent us here because the case was serious.'

My heart began to gnaw at me. What manner of man was Baboy? A man who could give a discourse on the Gita to Vasudev even as he had just admitted his own grandchild to the hospital in a critical state!

'Do one thing,' said Baboy, 'Just go to Gogol's and tell Madhu to come. And go home directly from there. Your folks will be worried about you.'

'You don't have to worry about me!' Involuntarily, my tone must have acquired an edge. Baboy looked at me and met my gaze. I saw the flicker of uncertainty in his look but it was only momentary.

'I will bring Madhu. But what about you?'

'I will wait here. The attendant will come soon. Besides, I like the ambience here. Friends and strangers, our elderly ancestors, they are all here—I could spend hours among them.'

Without waiting to hear more, I went to the car and wept till I reached Gogol.

I wept, not for the little child…but…I myself did not know why I wept—perhaps because I could feel Madhu's grief.

Baboy's brother Keshav was at home. The moment the car stopped, he came out of the house and I brought him up to date on the situation. He readied himself to come along with Madhu. Then Keshav's wife came out. She put some flowers in my hand. I couldn't count the numerous creases on her frowning forehead. Before taking that lifeless body into the house, Baboy should have thought about the disruption a dead body would cause to this orthodox family.

Madhu once again lifted the body gently.

On the way, I learnt the whole story from Keshav. The child had had diarrhoea for the last two days. Perhaps for fear of displeasing Baboy, they did not take him to a doctor immediately. When they finally took him, the doctor had ordered his immediate hospitalization.

Displeasing Baboy? Why? Why should Baboy tie others to his own likes and dislikes? Because he did not use soap, was it right of him to decree that no one else in the house should use soap? Who should decide whether the child should be given tinned milk or cow's milk? The mother, or the grandfather?

'I'm amazed that Baboy, who'll blow up any amount of money without batting an eyelid, just to sample a mutton dish that's been recommended, can hesitate so much before buying medicines or going to the doctor!' said Keshav, wiping his moist eyes.

The Baboy who gave a tenner to the shop-attendant boy with instructions not to tell anybody about it, swam before my eyes. That Baboy and this one!

His philosophy? To hell with it!

The crematorium attendant had not yet returned but his wife was there. 'I will dig the grave myself, Sir,' she offered.

'I will ask you if necessary,' Baboy told her.

The spot was selected and Baboy himself began to dig the grave. 'Do you ever work in the garden?' Baboy asked conversationally.

I shook my head.

Madhu was hugging the child and sobbing silently, almost as if he'd been warned: 'No crying!'

'One should dig a little every morning. You feel fresh the whole day long. It's good for health, too!'

I walked some distance away and squatted dejectedly on the ground.

The grave was ready.

A sob escaped Madhu. Gently, he placed the tiny body in the grave and arranged flowers on top of it. Then, he scooped earth over it. Baboy shovelled the mud in with his bare hands. The attendant's wife was wiping her wet eyes on her sari pallu.

Baboy was saying, 'There's one problem, though. Hyenas may come here at night. A heavy stone should be placed on top of the grave.'

Keshav brought one.

'We need a bigger one,' declared Baboy and started scouting around. 'Do you know that hyenas can dig up graves like humans? That's why we need a heavy stone.'

Baboy wandered off behind a clump of bushes. Since he was taking his time, I went looking for him. I found him, screened by the bushes, his face covered by a handkerchief, trying to stifle his sobs. I tiptoed my way back.

Baboy came back immediately. 'Over there, there's a big stone. But we won't be able to carry it.' Turning to the woman, he instructed, 'Please tell your husband to carry it over and place it on top of the grave. Here's five rupees. I will come later and check! The hyenas must not even get a whiff of the body, understand?'

She's Dead!

'How pleasant!' remarked Madkaikar, admiring the pinkish evening glow of Delhi as he stepped on to the ramp which had been wheeled to their plane. D'Souza, buttoning up his jacket, said, 'It's only five o'clock now—wait for the night and then you'll miss your wife!'

'Forget it!' replied Madkaikar, nudging D'Souza as they entered the Indian Airlines coach. 'Coming here and remembering one's wife is like going to the Oberoi and ordering rice and curry!'

Both of them laughed. They felt rather free with each other here—something they could not afford to be back home. In Goa, you can't laugh and joke with one another when you belong to opposing political parties. One has to be careful of what one says. Here you could even swap risqué jokes and nobody would understand their Konkani. You could even laugh loudly without any risk of anybody remarking, 'Just see how our State Minister guffaws in public!' Reflecting on this, Madkaikar burst into laughter.

'What's so funny?' D'Souza asked.

'Nothing... Today Palam seems different, doesn't it? All decked up. Some VIP must be coming,' remarked Madkaikar, surveying the airport.

'What do you mean? Aren't we VIPs?' quipped D'Souza.

'Not that. I mean VVIPs like the PM or some foreign dignitary.'

'My dear man, this is Palam, the airport of India's capital. VIPs and VVIPs keep coming and going every day.'

They chatted away in the car till they reached Goa Sadan. D'Souza had been allotted a separate room, but Madkaikar impulsively pulled him into his suite and dumped his luggage there.

Even though he'd had a bath before leaving his house, Madkaikar had another shower, which made him feel like a new man—almost as if he'd moulted out of his old skin! 'I feel ten years younger!' he remarked in English, brushing his hair.

Admiring his sleek, undyed black hair, his smooth complexion and the sparkle in his eyes, D'Souza said in Konkani, 'In fact you do look ten years younger.'

Noting that even an English remark elicited a Konkani response from D'Souza, Madkaikar couldn't help remarking, 'Funny! You normally speak English in Goa, but here you speak nothing but Konkani!'

D'Souza nodded his head in agreement, 'Here in Delhi, one Goan communicates with his fellow Goan in Konkani.'

'Why so?'

Momentarily nonplussed, D'Souza said, 'In Goa, everybody knows Konkani, but here, many speak English and almost no one knows Konkani. That is why it feels good to speak Konkani.'

Had D'Souza made such a statement in the Assembly, Madkaikar would have ripped him to shreds. But things happen differently in life—such indiscretions are uttered by ministers and the opportunity of chopping them up goes to the Opposition—a job that D'Souza was particularly good at. (He waits for the merest chance to pounce...) But forget politics for today. Once the conference begins tomorrow, there will be plenty of it. Tonight at least, one should be free of such tensions.

There was a discreet knock.

'Come in.'

The Commissioner walked in with a file under his arm. A crease of dismay appeared on Madkaikar's forehead. Seeing D'Souza there, the Commissioner hesitated. Knowing that this was because he belonged to the Opposition, D'Souza began to get up.

'Sit!' commanded Madkaikar, pushing D'Souza back into his seat. Telling the Commissioner that they would talk business the next morning, he sent him back.

'Business first,' D'Souza mock-admonished him.

'Look here, D'Souza, I don't want business today—that's for tomorrow.'

'Okay, Baba! But what will the Commissioner say?'

'What will he say? Irresponsible! But haven't you always been saying that in the Assembly?' Madkaikar laughed.

'Do I say it without cause?' countered D'Souza.

'With way too much exaggeration!'

'So you do agree!'

'Now, now, don't go catching me out—haven't I told

you that there will be no politics tonight? No arguments. Tonight I am not a minister and you are not the Leader of the Opposition. We are friends!'

D'Souza fell silent. But, then, Madkaikar usually tended to be refreshingly childlike.

Only recently, since he'd become a minister with the responsibilities of the job and the constant carping of the Opposition, Madkaikar had become a little subdued. But today, he had the innocence and vitality of a twenty-year-old. D'Souza saw a different personality in him and, for the first time, he felt a certain empathy with Madkaikar... I hurt him needlessly all this time and once, for a minor error, I even called him a fool. The poor guy would take all my needling without a word... Once, it was said, after a haranguing from me, he even sobbed in his cabin... D'Souza mentally resolved not to trouble Madkaikar too much in the future. This gentle fellow should not be pilloried for the CM's fault. After all, he was a minister only for cosmetic effect. Everybody knew that no minister's file could move up without the approval of the CM.

'What are you staring at me for?' Madkaikar demanded as he struggled into a pullover.

D'Souza shook his head.

'I know! You're wondering how I got into politics.'

Amazingly enough, this was the very question which had cropped up in his mind,

D'Souza laughed and nodded.

'Actually, I am myself surprised. I never had respect for politicians, nor a hankering for politics. I wanted to become a doctor, but didn't manage the qualifying percentage. I might still have got into medical college, but we didn't have the necessary political contacts, so that was that. After my BSc, I decided to do law.' Madkaikar smiled, wryly adding, 'Isn't a lawyer too, called "doctor" in Goa!'

'But how did you come into politics from law?'

'I was drafted into it... There was no one in politics from our caste, so our community made a representation to the CM. They needed an educated person, so my name was proposed. I was game. The minute I was elected, I was propelled into the Cabinet.' Tying his shoelaces, Madkaikar straightened up. 'Actually, I was supposed to become a full-fledged Cabinet minister—the CM had committed himself to it. But one minister had to be a Christian and Fernandes was adamant that he would settle for nothing less than Cabinet rank and so my Cabinet rank went to him.'

Madkaikar was already dressed. D'Souza looked at his watch. It was past seven, but they were in no hurry. 'Don't mind my asking, but you know Madkaikar, one doesn't remain a minister for ever—one goes, another comes—I mean, tomorrow you may not be a minister. What then? Politics or law?'

'Before contesting these elections, Mira had asked me the same question.'

'Mira? Your wife?'

'Yes, she kept pestering me to forget about the elections.'

'Thinking of the future?'

'Yes. I told her that we would cross our bridges when we came to them.'

'Next time, do listen to her advice. I must congratulate her.'

'Why?'

'For her timely and correct advice!'

'You mean I should have sacrificed my ministerial post and stuck to law?'

'Of course! According to what I heard, your practice was flourishing—you oughtn't to have given it up. But forget it. Tell me, what's the programme for tonight?'

'Very good! That's an important question. First, get ready, and then we'll go out. I want to enjoy the evening. In Goa I can't paint the town red. Tonight, we'll eat well, drink well and if we're in the mood for it...' Madkaikar touched his nose and winked.

'You bastard!'

'Swear in Konkani, man! You people keep cursing and complaining that the government does nothing for Konkani!'

'Right! But you forget that even those curses and complaints are in English!'

Both laughed heartily.

D'Souza washed his face, combed his hair and pulled on his jacket. 'Where shall we eat?'

'Which is Delhi's best joint?'

'You ask as if you don't know!' D'Souza tossed the query back into Madkaikar's court.

'Ah, come, you decide.'

'Okay. Ashoka?'

'No please. I feel out of place there.'

'Oberoi?'

'That's worse. Let's go to Connaught Place. Lido?'

'For God's sake, no! Three of the boys from the Lido band are from our village. Last year they told everyone that I drank a lot and the news even reached Mira's ears.'

'So? Does she disapprove of your drinking?'

'She says that I can drink at home but not elsewhere.'

'Very wise of her!'

'You can praise my wife later—now, where shall we eat? And not merely to eat, mind you!'

'Akbar?'

'I've never been there. Is it good?'

'Try it.'

'Okay, Akbar it is.'

As they were leaving, a messenger came running up to D'Souza, 'Sir, Sir, call from Goa!'

'Tell him.' D'Souza indicated Madkaikar.

'No, no, call for Mr D'Souza. You were given a ring in your room but you weren't there, Sir.'

'Phone call for me?' D'Souza felt a sudden stab of apprehension as he wondered what could have happened.

'You lock up and join me later,' D'Souza told Madkaikar, hurrying downstairs.

'Hello! Hello! Yes, D'Souza speaking.'

'Mr D'Souza! Bhat here. Personal Secretary to CM.' Mercifully, the line was clear.

'What has happened?'

'Very bad news, Sir. Is Mr Madkaikar close by?'

D'Souza's eyes shot upwards. Madkaikar was on the landing at the top of the stairs, talking to the caretaker of Goa Sadan.

'He's upstairs. Shall I call him?'

'No! No! Mr D'Souza, Madkaikar's wife met with an accident a short while ago!'

'What?'

'Accident! Hello! Can you hear me?'

Controlling his breathing, D'Souza said, 'Go on.'

'Serious accident! Fatal! Break the news to him gently— we leave it to you—and arrange to bring him back as soon as possible.'

'You mean she's...?'

'Yes, she did not survive, Mr D'Souza. Get a grip on yourself and look after him.'

Nodding wordlessly, D'Souza replaced the receiver. He looked up. Madkaikar was still talking and laughing as he apparently exchanged a joke with the caretaker.

Though it was cold, D'Souza was sweating profusely. He shivered when a cold breeze evaporated some of his perspiration. On the pretext of relieving himself, he went into the restroom. Supporting himself against the locked door of the toilet, he thought back on the day's events.

Madkaikar's wife, who had come to see her husband off at the airport that morning, appeared before him. Her delicate, graceful features seemed to be mocking him...at first gently, but growing ever more frightening... Suddenly, red kumkum began to pour from her forehead and, in no time, she was drenched in blood!

D'Souza wiped his forehead. He bent over the basin, washed, and then straightened up. He bent down once more and splashed water on his face again and again. No, he couldn't break the news to Madkaikar all at once; he would suffer a terrible shock. But how should he do it? Should he tell Madkaikar about his wife's death out there, in the car? No. Should he take him to the garden and tell him there? No. Or in the restaurant? Not there! Later…after dinner? No. Such terrible news!

He couldn't take a decision, so he decided to go out with an expressionless face and wait for the right opportunity.

Madkaikar was waiting expectantly. Before getting into the car, he said enthusiastically, 'I found out from the caretaker—he agrees that the Akbar is the perfect joint for us.'

D'Souza pitied him. His wife was lying dead in Goa and here this man was, working up an appetite!

D'Souza settled in the car in silence and Madkaikar got in beside him.

'Akbar chalo, driver.'

'No, first we'll go to Rajghat or to Shanti Van.'

'What for?'

'I find the atmosphere at Gandhiji's shrine peaceful'

'In this biting cold? You must be crazy!'

'Not that… It's not yet eight… What's the hurry?'

'For goodness sake! I'm ravenous. Do you realize that we haven't eaten a thing since lunch?'

'I'm not hungry. Let's eat here.'

'Not me, brother! It's been a long time since I've had a real appetite. Don't irritate me. By the way, what's the matter? You look changed.'

'What can the matter be?' D'Souza tried to mask the turmoil in his mind.

'Whose call was that? Your wife is okay, I hope?'

'Eh!' D'Souza hid his anguish again .

'What was that call about? Party affairs?'

D'Souza nodded dumbly

'You ought to have told them: No business today. Tomorrow...'

'Will you listen to me? Let's...'

'No, Sir! Right now, my belly is on fire. Later, I'll listen to anything you say, okay?'

No, he couldn't tell him now. The poor guy wouldn't be able to eat anything after hearing the news. No, he would let Madkaikar eat first and only then would he gently break the news to him.

'Okay.'

The Akbar was packed, but they managed a table in a corner.

The lights were soft. To D'Souza, the atmosphere felt forebodingly dark.

'Superb lighting effects, eh?' Madkaikar wasn't even interested in D'Souza's reply.

The live music—grating on D'Souza's ears—sounded discordant, and the singer seemed to be wailing a tuneless dirge.

Madkaikar's fingers were drumming on the table

appreciatively and his feet tapped in time to the music. 'What will you drink?' Madkaikar asked D'Souza as the waiter approached.

'No drinks, please.'

'I will not listen to you today! You know that I don't drink in Goa for two reasons—first, it is unbecoming for a minister to drink in public; and secondly, because Mira dislikes it.'

'That settles it then!'

'Why? Because Mira dislikes it? Forget it. You know, Mira had wanted to come to Delhi with me, but I said no. If she had come, then there'd be no fun. I couldn't drink or move about freely.'

Over his protests, Madkaikar ordered beers.

Mira had wanted to come and Madkaikar had stopped her. If she had come, if only she had come, this terrible thing wouldn't have happened. But how was he to tell him?

As soon as their drinks arrived, Madkaikar raised his glass, 'Cheers! To what shall we drink?'

D'Souza was silent.

'To your lousy mood! Cheers!' Madkaikar raised his glass to his lips.

D'Souza took a tiny sip and his stomach churned. A stiff whisky would have suited him better. He could polish off half a bottle of Scotch in one sitting but he couldn't drink now, not at a time like this.

'Sorry, Madkaikar, I have an upset stomach.'

Madkaikar downed half the glass in one draught.

'What! You won't even drink beer? Why did you take a
sip from that glass then? At least I would have drunk it!'
Madkaikar was getting irritated with D'Souza.

No! At least today Madkaikar should have refrained
from drinking... If only for the reason that his wife disliked
it...but how could D'Souza make him understand that...it
was merely for such trifling pleasures that this man had
not brought his wife along...and this had happened only
because he hadn't let her accompany him...

'Actually, I'm not much of a drinker. At the most I can
put away a beer or two and I don't drink whisky or
brandy—in fact, I'm yet to touch the stuff—when Mira
can't stand me drinking beer, where's the question of hard
liquor?'

'Finish your drink!'

'You think I'm high?'

In fact, the beer had barely started warming Madkaikar's
guts, but realizing that D'Souza would be bored sitting
and watching him drink, he said, 'I was thinking of having
another beer, but if you say enough, so be it—satisfied?
Now come on, order for food.'

D'Souza opened the menu, flipped through a few pages
perfunctorily, and tossed it to Madkaikar, thinking, I should
have told him the news before dinner. This guy deserves
to go hungry—he doesn't even think of his wife!

'What're you ordering?' Madkaikar asked.

'You decide.'

Surprised at D'Souza's uncooperative attitude, Madkaikar looked wonderingly at him. He shrugged and took up the menu.

'What's wrong with you today? Upset stomach?'

More questions would be asked were he to say no, so D'Souza nodded mutely. But the turmoil in him mounted. Looking up at Madkaikar's untroubled countenance, he felt a twinge of pity coupled with irritation. If he had to break the news to him, his own predicament at least would be at an end. But the poor guy must eat at the very least, otherwise till they reached Goa… Goa? When? How? He had to find out the details of the flight timings and make the arrangements.

'Tandoori?'

'No.'

'Fried fish? No, they must be using the frozen variety and not the fresh ones, right?'

'Look here, Madkaikar, I'm not feeling well and I'm just not hungry. Have whatever you want and have it quickly.'

Madkaikar was feeling good after the beer. He looked at the menu again, 'Fish and mutton are out…Mira's is the best and having it here would only spoil it for me. Yes. I think I'll settle for a chicken tandoori.'

Snapping the menu shut, Madkaikar told D'Souza, 'You know, tandooris are cooked best only by Punjabis; I must find a Punjabi cook in Goa and ask him to teach Mira to cook tandoori.'

Had he brought her to Delhi, she might have learnt. But now…

'Excuse me, I'll be back soon,' D'Souza got up.

Must have gone to relieve his upset stomach, decided Madkaikar.

D'Souza got the flight information. An Air India plane from Beirut would be touching down at Delhi en route to Bombay. That would be at one in the morning. The Bombay–Goa flight was at eight the next day, which meant that they would be home before ten in the morning. D'Souza phoned the Commissioner and asked him to book them both for Goa, and rejoined Madkaikar.

'Not angry with me, are you, because I had a drink? It's okay, but please don't raise it in the Assembly!'

D'Souza sighed.

'Why the hell are you sighing? I should be the one to complain, considering that you spoilt my evening!'

The chicken tandoori was served.

Seeing Madkaikar squirting lime juice on the red tandoori chicken on his plate, D'Souza shivered involuntarily. He imagined Mira's skinned leg on the plate and...

Madkaikar bent over the plate and sniffed the dish appreciatively. He inhaled the warm aroma of the grilled chicken deeply.

The smell nauseated D'Souza and he felt like going out for a breath of fresh air. But he killed his feeling of disgust.

'Sure you won't have any?' Madkaikar asked for the sake of formality, and started on the chicken. He ate with great relish, swaying gently to the music.

Watching Madkaikar take a chicken leg and attack it,

D'Souza held on to his mental reins even tighter, fighting for control.

Rinsing his fingers in a bowl, Madkaikar complained, 'You know, D'Souza, you ruined my evening. I'd planned to drink till I was tipsy, eat till I was satiated and, if you and I were in the mood for it, to top up the evening with… But you switched my mood off. Don't think that I don't know where you go and what you do when you come to Delhi alone. But because I'm with you…'

'Madkaikar!' D'Souza couldn't utter another word.

'Okay! Okay! You're a saint! You don't drink, you don't eat meat and you don't womanize. Get lost! I don't need you. I'm quite capable of doing everything on my own… I can… You want to see?'

'Madkaikar, please!'

'No! You have no right to ruin my evening. You know why I didn't bring Mira?'

'Don't take the poor woman's name!'

'What? Why this sudden affection for my wife? Don't tell me you're in love with her!'

Madkaikar had just started to laugh at his own joke when D'Souza's open palm struck his left cheek. 'Shut up! Do you know what's happened to your wife? She's dead!'

Coinsanv's Cattle

Driving his cattle before him, Inas herded them into the shed where he tethered them for the night. He entered the house by the back door. Bent over the fireplace, Coinsanv was coaxing the fire into life by patiently blowing on the embers. Hearing Inas coming in, she asked in surprise, 'Haven't you tied the cows yet, Inas?'

'I've just come in after tying them,' mumbled Inas shortly, sitting down on the box by the wall. Retrieving the butt of the viddi stuck above his ear, he held a lighted match to its tip and drew in the smoke deeply.

'Strange! Then why aren't they lowing today?' Coinsanv asked in wonder. Invariably, the cows would set off a continuous mooing after being tied up in the shed. And here was Inas, back in the house after tying them up, and they were still silent!

'They dare not open their mouths!'

'Why? What happened?' Coinsanv asked with a stab of apprehension. 'Did they enter someone's garden or…'

'Not in anybody's garden. They got into Paulu-bhatkar's coconut grove. They chewed some of his saplings, it seems. He threatened to impound them unless I paid him fifteen rupees. Only after I pleaded with him and promised to work on his plot did he let them go.'

Coinsanv heard him out in silence. Warming the tea that she'd brewed in the afternoon, she poured out a mug and placed it in front of Inas. The cattle were still quiet.

'Bitter... Like poison!' muttered Inas, grimacing distastefully after taking a sip of the smoky, stale black tea.

But Coinsanv was too preoccupied to pay attention to his grumbling. Why are the cattle still not mooing? How could they still not be hungry!

'Did the cows destroy many coconut saplings?'

'Nonsense! Not a single one! I doubt that they even touched a single leaf!'

In that case! In a trice Coinsanv realized what had happened. 'Inas, did you by chance vent your anger with the landlord on the animals?'

Inas' sullen silence was answer enough.

Leaving whatever she was doing, Coinsanv rushed to the cowshed. Both the cow and the bull were standing mutely. Normally, they would both lick her with their rasping tongues as soon as she walked into the shed. Today they made no such move. For a moment, Coinsanv imagined that they were averting her gazes! Could they be angry? Coinsanv laid both her hands on each of their backs. Immediately, they both started trembling. The cow started mooing first, followed immediately by the bull. Coinsanv started stroking the cow's neck with one hand and, with the other, she gently scratched the bull's forehead. The cow responded by licking her hand.

Coinsanv's glance roved over the animals minutely. Though there were no welts on their bodies, Coinsanv's experienced eyes could tell exactly where each stroke of the lash had landed. The animals were now continuously lowing in unison. They were famished. Patting them, Coinsanv coaxed them gently, 'Okay, okay, quiet now.' She then went to the house. Inas was outside readying the coconut fronds for thatching.

'Inas, is there any oilcake in the house?'

Inas maintained a stoic silence. In any case, what could he do? Whose stomachs was he supposed to fill? Three children. With their precarious hand-to-mouth existence, all they could think about was getting through each day. As long as the cow was yielding milk, they could afford to buy oilcakes. Last year they had a pair of bullocks which they used for ploughing. But, at Christmas, the black bull had died. Had it not died, they would have earned something from ploughing. Now, how could they afford oilcake for a cow gone dry and an idle bull?

'There's a little bran in the house, Inas. I'll go and collect some dhonn. Don't go out.'

By the time she made the rounds of their four Hindu neighbours, collecting the slop that they kept for her, the Angelus bells were ringing. She had barely entered the house, balancing the earthen pot on her head, when the cows set off an insistent bellowing.

Lowering the pot, Coinsanv put her hand in a bag and drew out some bran that she'd saved. She equally distributed the bran between two kodhim. Pouring the slop into both the earthen vessels, she stirred it with her hand till the bran was soaked.

The cattle were still lowing ceaselessly. Inas came out. Flicking the butt of his viddi, he got to work. Taking an old broom, he quickly cleared away the area in front of the cows. As soon as Coinsanv had finished stirring, he lifted the feed containers and placed them in front of the cattle. They began to eat greedily.

Coinsanv went to the well and drew a pitcher of water. By this time, the cattle had licked the containers dry. Pouring water into them, Coinsanv went inside. Outside, the children could be heard raising a ruckus. The pot was bubbling on the fire. Inas must have kept the rice water to boil while she'd gone to collect the slop. Mentally thanking him for his thoughtfulness, Coinsanv resumed her interrupted chores.

She roasted some dried sardines on the embers. After removing them from the coals, she sprinkled the last few drops of coconut oil from the bottle. The aroma that wafted up was appetizing.

'O—o, Inas!' somebody from outside called out.

'Coming!' Inas replied from the back. By which time Pedru had already made himself comfortable on the balcão. Getting the whiff of the roasted salt fish, he joked, 'Coinsanv, I'm inviting myself to dinner here tonight!'

'Please join us! We have excellent fish today!' retorted Coinsanv.

'That's obvious from the aroma!' Pedru laughed as he lighted a viddi.

By then Inas came out.

'Where are the cattle, Inas?' Pedru's question made Coinsanv's heart skip a beat. What now? Had their cattle got into somebody else's compound too? Pedru's next remark allayed the fear.

'Day after tomorrow is the Purument Feast in Margao. I'll be taking my buffalo heifer to sell at the fair. I've come to see if you're planning to go too.'

After a moment's hesitation, Inas replied, 'No. You carry on.'

Logic was telling him to sell the cattle. A single bull was useless for ploughing and a cow that yielded no milk was expensive to look after. But prudence warned him to not do anything without consulting Coinsanv. She loved the animals dearly.

'Don't be foolish! Your bull is getting old. What will you do if he too dies?' asked Pedru, exhaling smoke.

Inas remained silent. Inside, Coinsanv listened intently. Pedru continued, 'I'm selling my heifer. If I get a good crop this year, I may buy another one next year. You decide about yours. But do remember that you'll get the best price only at this fair. In my opinion, you'd better sell both the cow and the bull. You can always buy cattle later.'

Pedru went off, yet Inas did not come in. Coinsanv must have heard every word that Pedru spoke, but he did not dare broach the subject with her.

Coinsanv called the children in to eat. She served them bits of the roasted salt fish along with the kanji.

'Coinsanv, I'll be back soon,' said Inas.

Coinsanv knew exactly where Inas was headed.

Reflecting on what Pedru had said, Coinsanv squatted in front of the fireplace.

One cow and a pair of bulls. How Coinsanv had doted on them! There was nothing that both she and Inas wouldn't do for them. They had even deprived themselves to feed the cattle. Despite this, one bull had died of snakebite exactly on Christmas Day. During the Carnival, the cow had stopped yielding milk. And now...

When fending for three children and two adults was itself an overwhelming task, can one afford to be emotional about animals? The spiralling prices... They were already in the last days of May and had not even thought about the transplanting of paddy which had to be done before monsoon, in June. Others had already germinated their seedlings. Some had already transplanted them, hoping for early rains. Both Coinsanv's paddy plots were still fallow. The neighbours kept asking her, 'When will you be sowing?' But where would she get so much money from? Seedlings, fertilizer, weeding—for all this she needed...yes. It was essential that they sowed in their field. It was only because they had cultivated last year that their children could at least have kanji this year. Otherwise they would...! They must sow... The rains were nearing... Day after tomorrow was the Pentecost fair where one had to stock up provisions for the rainy season!

Inas trooped in after a tot at the taverna. Coinsanv served Inas some kanji. Inas glanced into the kanji buddkulo. As Coinsanv readied to ladle out some more for him, Inas said he'd had enough. Coinsanv guessed that he'd said that because there was very little kanji left in the pot. But Coinsanv was not hungry and said, 'I've already eaten, Inas. You eat well. You have to work tomorrow.'

'Don't lie to me. Have that kanji!' said Inas gruffly, getting up.

Coinsanv sipped her rice gruel and got up. She cleaned up the fireplace and came out of the kitchen. The kids were fast asleep. Inas had squatted on the box and was puffing away.

'Inas, day after tomorrow is the Purument Feast.'

Inas sucked deeply on the viddi and exhaled, but remained silent. He was bothered by the same thoughts.

'You're taking the cattle, aren't you?'

Inas stiffened. Was Coinsanv goading him? Testing him?

Inas shook his head vigorously.

'What do you mean no? Are you mad?' She was speaking to Inas but was obviously trying to convince herself. 'How will we manage if we don't sell the cattle? Don't we have to sow the fields? Where will the money for the fertilizer, the seedlings, come from? From your father?'

Inas heard Coinsanv out in wonder. He had been thinking along the same lines, but hadn't said anything because of Coinsanv's feelings. Now Coinsanv was herself telling him this!

'Are you serious?' Inas croaked in disbelief.

'Is this the time for jokes? There's only tomorrow. On the day after, you take them at dawn. Do you want me to come along?'

'There's no need.' Inas was relieved. All along, he'd been hesitating to broach the subject but, now, Coinsanv was herself urging him to sell the cattle. He slept soundly. After Coinsanv blew out the light and went to bed, Inas was asleep and could not hear her bitter sobs.

Getting through the next day was hell. Early in the morning, Mari-Santan called out, 'Coinsanv, have you seen the sky? It looks like the monsoon is coming soon!'

'Maybe.'

'Aren't you transplanting?'

'We're transplanting after the feast.'

'You'd better hurry up! The rains are round the corner! Some people have already transplanted their rich. And, haven't you heard, people are queuing up for fertilizer? You better reserve yours fast!'

If in the morning it was Mari-Santan, Caitan came by at noon. 'Have you bought your paddy seedlings?'

'Not yet.'

'Do you want some?' Caitan asked.

'Do you have stock?'

'Not me. But Bebdo-Santan, the drunkard, has some for sale. If you need it, you better tell him now.'

'I'll speak to Inas about it.'

The cows had not been put out to pasture that morning. Coinsanv herself took them to graze in the evening. Taking out some money that she'd saved, she bought a kilo of oilcake. Earlier, with one rupee you could get a kilo of oilcake and a small tablet of bathing soap besides. Now soap had become precious and a rupee would not even buy a kilo of oilcake! Mentally cursing the greedy shopkeeper, Coinsanv soaked the cake in water. Asking Inas to remain in the house, she went to the houses of the neighbouring Hindus. At each house, she collected the slop and, barely controlling the tears welling up in her eyes, she told them, 'From tomorrow, we won't need the slop. We are selling the cattle in the morning!'

Ladling out a generous portion of feed for the cattle, Inas and Coinsanv went in. Both were heavy-hearted. They had brought up these two dumb animals like their own children. And now they had to sell them for the sake of their own stomachs.

It was a terrible night, full of turmoil for them both.

Coinsanv got up at the crack of dawn. She lit the fire and put the kettle on for tea. She went into the cowshed and, sitting with the cattle, cried her heart out. She got up when she sensed that Inas had woken up. Coinsanv poured out the tea and both of them sipped it in silence by the fireplace. Outside, the world was stirring. Filip, Hari and Pedru were supposed to be taking their cattle to the fair. As he was putting on his shirt, Inas told her, 'Coinsanv, go to our field and straighten out the ridges. And send a message to Bebdo-Santan that we'll need his seedlings. If it rains tomorrow, we can transplant the day after.' But Coinsanv was hardly listening.

Pedru arrived noisily. 'Hoi there, Inas!'

Inas went out through the back door, untied the animals, and herded them out of the shed. Coinsanv couldn't restrain herself. Rushing out of the house, she hugged the cow. The bull came up to her and started licking her calves. With that, the dam burst and Coinsanv cried a flood of tears.

'You get inside now!' muttered Inas gruffly.

Her leaden feet would not move and Coinsanv remained rooted to the spot she was standing upon. Inas tugged at the cattle. Since Pedru was almost out of sight, he stepped up his pace, straining at the ropes. Coinsanv sensed that the cow's hooves had become heavy and the cattle didn't want to go. Inas was actually having to drag them away. What Coinsanv wanted to say was, 'No, Inas! Don't take them!' but the words did not come. What broke out instead were uncontrollable sobs. She sank down to the ground and squatted on her heels.

As the sun came out brightly, Coinsanv got a grip on herself. It was over. She served breakfast to the children and went to the fields. With a hoe, she softened the soil and levelled it. She then straightened the ridges. Spending half a day there she went home. After lunch, she went to Santan's and booked some seedlings. She next went to the fertilizer shop and found out which was ideal. 'I'll collect it tomorrow, keep some for me,' she told the shopkeeper.

When she reached home again, she remembered her cattle. She became uneasy. Her feet took her to the cowshed. The empty shed oppressed her. She entered. Such wonderful animals! We should never have sold them.

Where did we get this awful idea? Our cattle were so loving, so gentle. If that stupid Pedru hadn't come that day, we wouldn't even have thought of it! Hurling two curses at Pedru, a couple at Inas, and cursing herself, too, Coinsanv got up. She then put rice in the pot boiling on the fire to make kanji. As she put it in, she consoled herself. Never mind; let the cattle go! At least we won't go hungry next year.

The sun had set and the lengthening shadows of darkness were casting their gloom in the house. Misgivings started assailing Coinsanv once again. She thought, It was this same cow's milk that nourished my children. By selling her milk, we could manage to buy provisions. This very bull helped maintain our household with his ploughing. And today we have decided to sell them! Our lovely cattle! God help us! I hope nobody buys our cow! I hope our bull comes back! Coinsanv consoled herself with these fervent pleas.

It was past Angelus: time for Inas to be back. But Coinsanv did not allow herself to go out and sit. Without even lighting a lamp, she squatted inside in the dark.

Quite often, many cattle come back unsold. But those cattle are quite different. Our animals are so loving; anybody will grab them. We should never have sent them! As she sat there with these thoughts tormenting her, she heard the distant tinkling of cowbells. Coinsanv stepped out.

Pedru was in front. Inas was trailing him. In the darkness she felt she could make out Pedru returning with his buffalo. But she had forgotten that Pedru's buffalo did not have a bell. Surmising that Coinsanv would be pleased even if the cows were not sold, Inas was coming back with the cows with a spring in his step.

A stunned Coinsanv was motionless for a moment. That fallow field, those seedlings, that fertilizer—everything began swimming before her eyes.

The cow had barely started licking her hand affectionately when Coinsanv began screaming: 'You whore! You wretched animals! How the hell are we to manage now? How are we to sow the field? What are we going to eat next year? Go—and die!' as she flailed with her hands at the two dumb animals.

Bandh

'I've seen lots of strikes, hartals and bandhs, but nothing like this!' grumbled Dattaram, entering the house after he had angrily jerked his motorcycle upright on to its stand. Flinging the ignition key onto the table, he threw himself on the bed without bothering to change his clothes.

In earlier bandhs, because buses and cars were off the road, motor-cycle pilots could make hay. During last year's general strike, Dattaram had pocketed a cool one hundred and seventy rupees in just half a day.

But today, things had been different. He had set out on his motorcycle-taxi earlier than usual. He'd barely left his neighbourhood when he noticed the first barricade. But it had not been enough to hold back a two-wheeler with an expert rider like Dattaram. He had coolly squeezed the bike through a narrow gap at the side and lifted it. Admiring his own skill, he had brought the bike back onto the road. Caetan, Peter and Suresh who had been standing there, stopped him, 'Where are you going Dattaram?' Caetan asked.

'To Margao bus stand.' Dattaram had thought that Caetan would ask him for a lift. And what if Peter, too, wanted to go triple-seat? He didn't mind giving Caetan a lift, but he had firmly decided that he wouldn't carry triple. But Caetan said, 'Don't you know that there's a bandh today?'

'I know. But motorcycles are exempted from bandhs, aren't they?'

'Today's bandh is for everybody. It is for the sake of our mother tongue,' Suresh had informed him.

Dattaram had hesitated a while, then, running his hand over his bike, he had pleaded, 'But it's my daily bread, let me pass.'

But his importuning had served only to embolden Caetan. 'Dattaram, you better go home. Going hungry one day won't kill you!'

Realizing that discretion was the better part of valour, Dattaram had turned homewards without another word.

In fact, Caetan and Peter were his companions. You could even call them friends.

Every Sunday evening, when he took a break from plying his motorcycle, he played football with this very Caetan. Whenever there was any problem in the neighbourhood or in the village, Dattaram and Caetan would generally set out together to try and sort things out. But today, Dattaram was angry with Caetan.

What were they trying to do? Enforce a bandh by show of force! If they wanted a bandh, they could stay at home; why deprive others of their livelihood? For the cause of language they claim. As if I don't want my language! Some people do oppose their own mother tongue. True enough. But why a bandh? And why use force to enforce a bandh?

Around ten-thirty, his neighbour Kalidas came calling. 'The signs of today's bandh don't seem to be good,' he remarked. Dattaram, who was already grumpy, nodded wordlessly. But Kalidas had not finished. 'I'm not talking about this place alone. Here, bandh-breakers are being beaten up. But over there, bandh-enforcers are on the receiving end, it seems! It's all set to blow up!' Kalidas hurried away to give some more people the benefit of his analysis.

A bandh to support a language? For God's sake! A language is meant to bring people together, not tear them apart! Language is a vehicle to foster understanding. It is meant to unite, not to divide people. But whom do we tell this to? Nobody is in a mood to listen. We can make people understand, but who's willing to listen? Dattaram was mumbling to himself. By eleven he had run out of cigarettes and he got up to go and buy a new pack.

When he reached the door, he realized that because of the bandh, all the shops and even the kiosks would be closed.

Dattaram changed his clothes. He went to the well for a bath. Only after pouring about eight pitchers of cool water over his head did the tension drain out of his body. When Caetan and Peter came looking for him, he was still at the well. On seeing the duo, Dattaram's irritation returned.

'Does your bandh also mean that I cannot have a bath?' he taunted.

Uncharacteristically, Caetan kept mum. After a moment's silence, he humbly said, 'Dattaram, I've come to ask you for a favour. Finish your bath; we'll wait at the entrance.'

A perplexed Dattaram quickly finished and went out to meet them.

'Dattaram, we have a guest. She has to be taken to Fatorpa and brought back,' said Caetan.

Dattaram was still angry. Wiping the water off his body, he said, 'Not me, brother. Today's a bandh!'

Peter intervened. 'Please, Dattaram! Nobody but you can help us.'

'I'll do the job willingly, but not today! Tomorrow,' said Dattaram, adding sarcastically, 'today we are observing a bandh for the sake of our mother tongue, aren't we?'

Swallowing the slight, Caetan beseeched him, 'Okay, man, please! People all over know you and nobody will stop you. That's why I've come to ask you this favour. I'll pay double the fare but don't say no to me. Please!'

'This morning, when I told you that I had to earn my daily bread, didn't you tell me to remain hungry? And now you're trying to bribe me by dangling the carrot of double-fare.'

Caetan took Dattaram's stinging rebuke in silence. He knew that Dattaram wasn't one of those people who could be bribed. He said in resignation, 'It's up to you. I came because I needed you. You know my cousin Rosy, don't you? She's teaching in Chandigarh. She'd come to Goa for a week's holiday. She's leaving today by the night train to Bombay. Before going she has to take some offerings of coconut and rice to the Fatorpa Temple. Since Goddess Shantadurga has cast her benevolent eye on her, Rosy is under an obligation to pay her a visit with her votive offerings before going back. That is why I have come to ask you... But if you can't... So be it.'

Dattaram hesitated. He had cooled down by now. He was reluctant to let go of the business that had come calling at his door. Over and above the fare that he would make, he would also earn goodwill and gratitude from Caetan. Dattaram wheeled the motorcycle out. Kicking the engine to life, he carried Caetan to his house.

Rosy was a young woman. She was pushing thirty but was not yet married—she was rather plain-looking and simple.

Caetan said to Dattaram in a low voice, 'I hear that there's trouble along the way! They're stopping traffic— but you'll manage to convince them.'

It was on the tip of Dattaram's tongue to ask, 'This morning, how willing were you to be convinced?' But, glancing at Rosy, he kept quiet.

Rosy mounted the pillion seat behind him. Just then, Rosy's mother came up to Dattaram. Putting her hand on Dattaram's arm, she said, 'Son, take care of my daughter and bring her back safely. May Our Lady bless you too!'

Dattaram engaged the gears, released the clutch, and set off. Dodging all the barricades, he reached the highway. Concrete electric poles were blocking the road at some places while at others, iron telephone posts had been laid across the path. Laterite stone, granite boulders, rubble—

virtually anything that served the purpose. By the time he reached Cuncolim, he had been stopped at least a dozen times but, every time, Dattaram's gift of the gab had seen them through. Soon after Cuncolim, a huge tree was blocking the road. Asking Rosy to get down, Dattaram managed to negotiate that barrier. Relieved that they would be in Fatorpa in less than ten minutes, Dattaram had barely got back on the road when, all of a sudden, a dozen men blocked his way. For a fleeting moment, Dattaram toyed with the idea of dodging them and darting forward. Then, deciding that it would be better to proceed with their permission, he halted.

'And, where do you think you're going, man?' a tall, hefty young man demanded.

Dattaram found his provocative tone objectionable. But, discretion being called for today, he replied in a calm voice, 'I'm going to Fatorpa.'

All the men moved close. 'Make them get down! The pillion rider first!' ordered a voice from the back.

'Allow us to leave,' Dattaram said as he lightly revved up the bike. Rosy lowered her hands from Dattaram's shoulder and clasped him tightly round the waist.

'You're not going anywhere!' the burly youth told him, brusquely removing Dattaram's hand from the throttle grip. Another young man placed his hand on Rosy's shoulder and asked, 'And who is this? Has she hired you or is she for hire?'

Dattaram was furious. Angrily turning around, he removed the man's hand from Rosy's shoulder. The man erupted. Grabbing hold of Rosy, he started to drag her down from the bike. Dattaram accelerated furiously and the bike leaped forward, pushing two of the men to the side. But, because Rosy was firmly in the boy's grip, Rosy fell off the seat straight into his arms.

Dattaram swivelled the bike around and rushed at the men. But when he reached them, they threw him off the motorcycle. They then attacked the bike and smashed its lights. Sizing up the situation, Dattaram contritely joined his hands and pleaded, 'She's my neighbour. Please let us go!'

The burly youth ordered, 'Okay, let him go. But we'll keep her!'

For a brief moment, Dattaram was tempted to leave. In the very next moment though, he saw Rosy's mother on one side and Shantadurga, the goddess of Cuncolim, on the other. Understanding his responsibility, he banished the thought.

Hearing Rosy scream, he snapped out of his trance. Someone had grabbed her blouse from behind and had torn it. Dattaram went berserk. Screaming abuses, he waded into the group of men, smashing whoever he came in contact with. Dattaram was receiving many blows to his legs, his back and even his head, but he was oblivious to them all.

Seeing the situation taking a serious turn, some of them ran—for reinforcements, Dattaram surmised. He caught hold of Rosy and told them between the hammering he was getting, 'She was going to pay her respects to

Shantadurga at Fatorpa. You have molested her. Remember that the Goddess won't forget what you've done!' The rain of blows waned somewhat.

Taking advantage of the lull, Dattaram lifted his vehicle. He kicked the bike to life and quickly got Rosy to mount behind him. Knowing that they were escaping, some men tried to stop them. But, deliberately charging at them with the engine revving full blast, Dattaram managed to escape.

Crouching behind him, Rosy was trembling and sobbing softly. On the way back, whoever tried to stop them would step back and let them pass seeing the sorry state they were in. Dattaram's shirt was in tatters, his forehead sported a big gash, one eye was black and swollen, both his knees and elbows were bleeding, but he was unmindful of it all.

He rode straight to Caetan's house, stopped at the doorstep, and dismounted.

Alarmed, Caetan ran up to them. 'What happened, Dattaram?'

Dattaram' eyes were bulging. He was speechless. Getting back on the bike, he started it. Finally finding his voice, he spat out: 'This is our language! This is our culture!'

The Vighnaharta

'Are you listening?' my wife called out. 'I was saying that chovoth is just around the corner. We have to observe the bare minimum at least, don't we?'

She was reminding me of the fast approaching Ganesh festival.

'What are you planning to do?' I asked, trying to keep the misgivings in my heart out of my voice.

'I'm not craving for anything grand but at least we have to make some sweets for the family.'

'We'll do what has to be done. But there are still some days to go,' I said, adding blandly, 'we'll see about it tomorrow.'

However, though I'd managed to hide the worry in my heart, my eyes must have given me away. My wife caught me by the sleeve and said, 'Your eyes are so strained! You worry over every little thing. As if I don't know the situation! I wouldn't even have mentioned it, but...'

Seeing her eyes well up distressed me.

'No... No... Savitri, you weren't wrong. It's perfectly true. Ganesh Chaturthi is just round the corner. We have to celebrate. But because of...this situation...I can't...'

Putting her hand to my mouth, Savitri prevented the sob from escaping hers. Her voice thick with emotion, she said, 'Please don't worry... God is great... Ganapati will...' and the rest of the words escaped along with her silent sigh. Savitri went inside while I slid on my sandals and came to the balcão.

Outside, the children were busy. The eldest, Suresh, was reading a story book borrowed from the neighbours, while Vimal, the third, was loudly reciting a poem. The middle one, Babush, sitting on the lower step and staring fixedly at a crow sitting on the branch above, was saying,

'Mr Crow, Mr Crow,
If we're getting guests today,
Stay on, stay on.
But if we're not,
Fly away! Fly away!'

The crow cocked his head towards Babush, stared at him quizzically for a brief moment, screeched 'Caw Caw!', flapped his wings, and flew away. For no logical reason, I felt relieved.

Forty years ago, I too, used to say the same thing to a crow. Having a guest was such fun! But today I dread guests. It's a shameful thing to admit, but nevertheless very true.

Descending the couple of steps from the house, I went towards Babush. He was staring in disappointment at the empty space from which the crow had flown. I hugged him and told him to do his homework. As I turned my back, he clutched at my shirt and said, 'Baba, you'll bring us some firecrackers today, no?'

'Of course, I will!' I lied feebly.

'And sparklers too!' Babush added with twinkling eyes.

'Yes, I will…' Before I could complete my answer, Vimal, who must have overheard, piped in, 'Baba, what about me? You better not forget me! I know how to light crackers now!'

'How could I forget my little darling? I'll bring crackers for everybody. Now come on, get on with your homework.'

And I set off.

Just before reaching the market I met Kushta. He never has a good word to say about anybody nor any good news to spread. Who has beaten up whom, where the recent fights have taken place, who has died and in what manner and who has cheated whom—this is Kushta's staple gossip.

'Hi there, Shankar! Did you hear the latest? João from Kondyaband has kicked the bucket!'

'Poor fellow. But he was ailing for some time, wasn't he?' I said perfunctorily.

But Kushta had plenty more. 'He fell sick only recently. If you ask me, he was murdered by his family…'

I can't stand this sort of talk, so I interrupted, 'Come on, why do you…'

'You listen to me—call me a liar if you want! But Joao's son and daughter-in-law literally starved their father to death! Shi, Shi! Worms will feed on them! They used to beat him day in and day out and keep him hungry! If I'm lying, cut off my ear and dump it in your shit!'

I was in no mood to listen to Kushta's drivel, so I started walking away. Kushta put out his hand to detain me and asked bluntly, 'Is it true that your bill with shopkeeper Vishnu is pending? He was telling me. Not that it's any business of mine... But I thought I'd ask you if it was true.'

My eyes narrowed in irritation. I caught him by the arm and asked, 'Kushta, did Vishnu tell you this?'

'If he didn't tell me, how would I know? What a silly question!'

Abruptly leaving Kushta there, I headed straight for Vishnu's grocery. It isn't in my nature to tolerate such blatant insults! I'd rather starve!

When I reached the shop, I was a different person. I asked, 'Vishnu, have I ever cheated you?'

'Of course not. Why do you ask?' Vishnu seemed mildly surprised.

'Then why did you spread the news that I owe you money? Why did you tell Kushta? Did you have to spoil my name for the sake of a small bill?'

Vishnu, a seasoned businessman, was unfazed. Rubbing salt into my wounds, he said calmly, 'My dear Shankar, those who are thin-skinned and have a lot of pride should not run up debts. I haven't told any lies about anybody. I have merely spoken the truth.' His cool words burned into me. I marched straight to Desai, the coconut merchant. Deciding to sell the two hundred odd coconuts that I'd kept aside, I said to him, 'Desai-bab at what rate are you buying coconuts?'

'How many do you have?' he asked.

'Two hundred, but I want cash down.'

With the one hundred and twenty rupees that I received, I settled Vishnu's bill of ninety-five rupees and walked home in a temper.

All this time, I had hidden my anxieties because of my obsession with pride. Just as papers fly away when the weight holding them down is removed, all my worries took off as I walked homewards. My wife had told me to bring home a tin of baby formula. The baby was now a year old and needed a tin every week. But Savitri managed to stretch it. The last tin I'd bought was almost a fortnight ago, and it ran out only the day before yesterday. Yesterday, I pretended that I'd forgotten it but, today, I had to buy one. Without any further ado, I bought a tin of baby formula from a pharmacy.

I once again began the trek home. Babush was waiting anxiously for me at the door. 'Come on, Baba, hand over my crackers and sparklers. Quick!'

I pushed him aside gently, avoiding his gaze. I did not want to see his tears. I walked into the kitchen. Depositing the tin of milk, I sat down.

'Why did you bring the small tin? It's more expensive and it runs out quicker too!'

Looking Savitri in the eye, I said, 'The formula runs out quicker from a small tin, and money runs out faster if we buy the big tin.'

Savitri shot me a quick look, then turned back to the fire and began to tend it.

Pouring some tea, she placed a cup in front of me and said, 'Tomorrow morning, without fail, I have to make some nevreos. We won't have to spend much on those sweets. Thank God we have some coconuts saved.'

I was barely registering what Savitri was saying. How could I tell her that the coconuts were already sold?

And she was still talking...

Outside, Babush was howling because I hadn't bought any firecrackers...

And, in the cradle, the hungry baby was bawling away.

Savitri's painful talk continued, 'We'll need around twenty-five coconuts. You only have to buy the sugar, jaggery, white flour and wheat flour. We've nearly run out of rice, but we haven't yet collected our quota of ration rice. We'll bring that...'

Savitri was actually planning everything in the most penny-pinching way. But to even buy those things, the least I needed was forty rupees. Besides that, I still had to buy the idol of Lord Ganesh.

In as low a voice as possible, I ventured, 'But Savitri, so many nevreos... Twenty-five coconuts...'

Cutting me off, Savitri reminded me, 'Have you forgotten that we have to send a vojem for your newly married sister? We cannot avoid that!'

My eyes started receding into their sockets. How could we send the customary offering of sweets to my sister now? Steeling myself, I said, 'Savitri, Savitri, we don't have any more coconuts now. I've sold them already!'

Savitri just couldn't take it. She kept squatting in front

of the fireplace and stared blankly at it. I got up, walked into the bedroom, and lay down on the bed.

Ganesh Chaturthi, the basket of sweets, the idol, firecrackers, sparklers, nevreos, rice, sugar—how on earth was I going to manage with just twenty rupees in my pocket! Besides...

Savitri tiptoed into the room. Running her hand gently over my forehead and through my hair, she said soothingly, 'Don't worry about anything... Leave everything to God. The Vighnaharta will solve our problems too.'

'Savitri, there is no God! This is the kingdom of the Devil. If there was a God, we wouldn't be having all these problems!'

'Hush there! Please don't blaspheme. He will not like it.'

I could not sleep all night. Chovoth, the basket of sweets, the Ganapati idol and the firecrackers kept parading in my head like characters on a stage. Though I'd paid off Vishnu's bill, it had come at the cost of severing relations with him. I just couldn't go to his shop again. I didn't feel like going to Gaonkar's shop either. But beggars, as they say, can't be choosers. I decided to visit him the next day. Who knew, some virtuous action of some ancestor of mine chalked up in the Lord's book of good deeds might just induce Gaonkar to sell to me on credit. In which case, we could manage to get through the festival season. But what if he didn't? The question was daunting, but, there was no escaping Ganesh Chaturthi.

If only the festival were a month hence, we could

have managed with the sale of coconuts from the harvest which was due next month. Or, we could have avoided the celebrations if we were in the middle of the Suver or the Sutak, the twelve-day period following child-birth or death in the family. But it was silly to even think about it!

In the middle of the night, Babush began chanting loudly in his sleep, 'Ganapati Bappa Morya; Fuddlya Vorsa Yenvya.'

Even at that late hour, I felt like laughing at the irony of it. Babush was waiting for the Ganesh festival with great longing and I was dreading it and hoping for ways to avoid it! But, can you avoid the chovoth festival? Can you neglect to send the vojem of sweets? Can you avoid making the nevreo sweets, buying the traditional fireworks and, of course, the mahurt, the idol of Ganapati—all were absolutely unavoidable.

Deciding to visit Gaonkar the next day, I invoked Nidra, the sleep-goddess, and the wife of Kumbhakarna, the mythical brother of Ravana.

The next morning, I walked with misgivings to Gaonkar's shop. It's not in my nature to stomach anybody's rebuff and I hoped that Gaonkar would oblige me. Savitri had claimed, 'Lord Ganesh will take care of our problem.' We'd come to know now! By the time I reached the shop, I was in a cold sweat.

There were some customers at the shop. They all left one by one after being served. I waited till everybody had gone. I could hear my heart thudding. My throat felt dry.

The entire future of my Ganesh festival hinged on Gaonkar. Bracing myself, I stepped forward.

'Gaonkar-bab,' I greeted, steeling myself.

'Hello there Shankar-bab! You've been standing there for quite a while. What can I do for you?'

With hope, I said, 'I've come to ask you for a favour. I need some things for Chaturthi. I'll be plucking my coconuts in another three weeks and I'll pay you as soon as I they are sold. Please don't refuse me. I'd be greatly indebted.' I spoke in an entreating tone.

'Don't misunderstand me Shankar-bab, but I'm sorry. We ourselves are not in good financial shape these days.'

The festival seemed to be mocking me right in front of my eyes. Without waiting to hear any more, I took off from the shop. Ganapati, the Great Solver of All Difficulties, my foot! Did she say that He would take care of our problem! And we are supposed to venerate such a God!

I left the place with patently disappointed eyes. Coming onto the road, I saw Kushta coming my way. I should have been spared this encounter!

'Hi there, Shankar!' he said, coming close. 'So you won't be celebrating Ganesh Chaturthi this year, right?' Before I could register what he was trying to say, he elaborated, 'You don't seem to have heard. That elderly Zayu-akka passed away early this morning. She's a distant aunt of yours, isn't she?'

'What's that? Did you say that she died? That means Sutak...?' The realization that we now had to observe the compulsory mourning period left me light-headed.

'Of course, Sutak! All twelve days of it!'

Kushta had, as usual, been the traditional harbinger of bad news, but I'd never heard better news from his mouth! The idol, chovoth, the basket of sweets, firecrackers—all started fleeing away one by one! And I was overcome by immense relief.

Teresa's Man

Sleep has fled Peter's eyes long ago but the lethargy in his body does not permit him to even turn on his side. The early morning cold makes him shiver but he is too lazy to pull up the sheet. The sound of splashing water tells him that Teresa must be in the bathroom. Peter is irritated. My job is to fill up that big copper bhann—and it is her privilege to drain it! He dare not voice his thoughts, though, because it would draw this retort from Teresa: 'Yes! Just as it is my job to earn the money and your privilege is to spend it!'

Teresa enters the bedroom. Peter looks at her through sleepy eyes. Teresa is in a camisole which sticks to the wet parts of her body. Taking a long wooden rod, she reaches for a towel from the clothesline, strung up high. As she stretches her arms, the petticoat armholes open to reveal…! Peter shuts his eyes. He looks again. With the upward movement of her arms, her slip has ridden up her legs, exposing a generous portion of her thighs. Like the tender white inner trunks of banana suckers, Peter thinks, gaping. He is aroused and wide awake now.

Teresa wipes her face and neck. The uneven texture of the towel leaves her fair skin slightly flushed.

Her mother-in-law is in the kitchen making tea, noisily banging the pans. She believes that since even a finger can dent aluminium, there was no point in being careful. Teresa has stopped wincing at the noise, philosophizing that she can't afford to buy stainless steel utensils—not in this life at least. Peter, of course, keeps quiet, reasoning that since he does not contribute to the kitty, he has no right to comment.

'P-e-d-r-u!' yells Teresa.

Other wives fondly anglicize their husbands' names—Antonio, for example, is called Tony; and Vitorino becomes Victor. But this woman insists on calling poor Peter 'Pedru'. Peter resents it acutely! But is she bothered?

'It's nearly eight, Pedru!'

Peter is irritated. Can't she wake up earlier? This is becoming a habit with her.

'Get up! Get up, Pedru! It is time for the train. Drop me to the station. Quick!' Striding towards him, she stamps her feet and pulls him by the hand. 'Get up you lazy man! If I miss the train, *you* won't take the boss's firing!'

Peter reluctantly gets out of bed and shuffles to the bathroom. He splashes cold water on his eyes to cool his rising temper. Finishing, he comes inside, angrily pulls on his trousers, shrugs himself into a shirt and grumbles, 'I can't even sleep in peace. Why can't she get up earlier and walk to the station?'

But Teresa must have heard him grumbling. She walks up to Peter and berates him. 'Admirable courage you have to grumble! You shameless idler! All you do is sit at

home and eat. Is it too much to just drop me by cycle to
the station once in a while when I'm late? Does it strain
your back? I work all day to feed you, only to take crap
from you people! I tell you, I'm fed up of you all. I've
ended up in hell after marrying you!'

'You wanted a love marriage, didn't you?' A voice
from the kitchen calmly adds fuel to the fire.

Her mother-in-law's gibe is more than she can take.
Teresa breaks into a sob and her eyes well up with tears.

In a better mood now, Peter slips on his sandals, gulps
down his tea, and is ready to leave. The tip of Teresa's
nose now competes with her cherry-red blouse. Even her
ear lobes are scarlet. She's wearing a tight skirt that fits
snugly round her hips. Peter's frown deepens in disapproval
of her figure-hugging skirt and sleeveless blouse. He wheels
his cycle out. Mounting it, he puts one foot on the pedal,
the other on the threshold and waits for Teresa. This was
how he used to wait for her at the station two years ago.
He used to be in love with her then...

'What's the problem now? Hurry up!' Peter bellows.

High-heeled shoes clicking smartly on the cement floor,
Teresa comes out of the house and sits on the cross-bar of
the bicycle. As they move, Teresa's memory goes back to
those days...

Peter would patiently wait for me with his cycle early
in the morning outside my house to give me a lift to the
station. Without fail. Every day. Over my protests. A
funny thing had happened one day. He had arrived early
in the morning, as usual, and had started taking his

customary laps on the bike round my house. Having come at seven-thirty and, on seeing no sign of me till eight-thirty, he had begun to get anxious. Just then, I returned from Mass. On seeing me he'd hurried to my side and asked, 'You haven't yet gone to office today, Teresa!' Barely stifling a laugh, I'd said, 'Today is Sunday, isn't it?' How comic he'd looked then!

The memory makes Teresa laugh. Her laugh annoys Peter. Wasn't this the same Teresa who was sobbing just a while ago? And now she's giggling. What could have made her laugh? She's probably thinking about someone in office! So was the weeping at home just play-acting?

As they neared the station, they see that the train is already at the platform. Peter instinctively pedals desperately and screeches to a halt at the end of the platform.

'P-h-i-r-r!' A shrill whistle sounds as the guard flags off the train. Leaping off the cycle, Teresa bounds away, clutching her bag tight. Running along the platform, she grabs hold of the hand-rail at the entrance of a carriage as the engine starts with a long toot. The train pulls away with Teresa hanging on. She makes a feeble attempt to climb in but her tight skirt hampers her. Alarmed, she hangs on to the bar for dear life as the train gathers speed. An alert man standing near the door sees her predicament and, putting his arm round her, he pulls her in. She doesn't even glance in Peter's direction. But Peter sees her smiling and thanking her young saviour.

'Quick-witted fellow to pull her in like that! Fast reactions!'

'Lucky guy! He enjoyed that!'

'And so did the girl! Why else do they go to work?'

'That's a fact. Once you have a job, you can have all the fun you want and nobody will question you!'

Peter is seething with rage at the comments made by the onlookers on the platform. He wants to slap them, but there are four of them. Forget it!

He sets off on his bicycle, furious. Why can't she leave a little earlier? Must she wear those ridiculously tight skirts? It's fine for her, but *I* have to face the snide remarks from those louts. And that gigolo who pulled her in with his arm round her waist... He must have enjoyed it... Didn't those chaps call him a lucky man. And Teresa? 'The girls enjoy it. Why else do they go to work?' is what they said. Enough is enough! I'm going to tell Teresa—no more work and no more tight skirts!

In fact, soon after their marriage, Peter had made it clear to Teresa that he did not approve of her wearing those tight-fitting skirts, but Teresa said that, as a receptionist, she was expected to be smartly turned out. One thing, though, is that she never wears such clothes in the house. Secretly, Peter wants her to wear body-hugging minis with daring sleeveless tops for him at home, but not to office. But Teresa doesn't, assuming that Peter would disapprove. Poor Peter doesn't have the courage to tell her what he really wants.

'Peter!' Guilherme calls out. Peter would have cycled on but he's heard that Guilherme's father has come down for good from East Africa only yesterday. He is curious to see what stuff he's brought, so he turns his cycle around. Guilherme's dad, in a colourful kitenge shirt favoured by Africa-returned Goans, is relaxing in an easy chair in the hall.

'It's Peter, isn't it? How are you?' He gets up and shakes hands with Peter. 'So how are things? What are you doing now?' he asks with a foreign accent.

'Business.' The reply springs to Peter's lips, but he swallows it.

Usually, Peter puffs out his chest and says, 'Business.' And if anybody probes further with, 'What business?' he has a stock reply too, 'All sorts of business—when the price of coconuts goes up, I trade in coconuts; during the watermelon season, I deal in watermelons; and, when nothing else is available, I even buy and sell fish.'

In actual fact, Peter has never done any business in his life. Ever since he scraped through the High School SSC exam, he's worked just twice. The first was as a counter salesman in a pharmacy. It involved getting up early and cycling to Margao town. Soon after lunch, he had to rush back to work without his customary siesta. He would reach home well after eight in the night. The routine did not quite appeal to his indolent nature and, one day, after a dressing down from his boss for reporting late, he never went back. He didn't even bother to claim his wages for the thirteen days that he had worked there. He decided that he would tell his mother, and whoever asked him, that he was going into business. He slipped Teresa the same line before getting married and, being deeply in love with him, she not only believed him, but was infinitely proud of him!

He had taken his second job for the sake of Teresa, once they were married. Teresa had cajoled her boss into giving Peter a job. Peter started work in a different department of the same company against his wishes. It meant getting up early, catching the train, rushing to office and writing with a pen the whole day long without a siesta of even five minutes after lunch. Wrestling with strange words like 'freight', 'demurrage', 'filing' 'checking slip', 'statement', 'consignment' gave him fever one day. The fever was a good enough excuse and he never went back.

'You're doing nothing at all?' Guilherme's father has seen through him. 'You should work! At least join the ship!' His words are like bitter medicine in his throat. 'How do you manage without a job?'

'His wife works,' Guilherme pipes up helpfully, rubbing it in.

'What? You remain idle and send your wife to work? Very bad! What sort of a man are you?' he exclaims. 'Never do that, my boy,' he adds paternally, 'or she'll get too big for her boots. Women should be shown their place. A man should...' He stops as Guilherme's mother comes in.

Peter decides it's time to leave. The truck with the luggage is expected any time. Lest he be asked to help unload it, Peter hurriedly takes their leave, picks up some fish at the village market, and goes home.

'You've arrived just in time. I was hoping that you'd come.' Peter's mother greets him.

Silently picking up a pitcher, he goes to the well and begins to fill up the empty utensils. From past experience he knows that were he to baulk, it would only draw a sharp retort from his mother: 'Why can't you help? You're doing nothing as it is!' To which he would have no reply.

He lies down on the cot to take a nap, but he cannot sleep. Venomous little suspicions crowd his mind. What is Teresa doing at that moment? Giggling in the office? With the boss perhaps? Or the character who lifted her into the train? Who was the guy? She must know him. How well? Teresa's sleeveless top, her tight skirt, the way he lifted her in with his arm around her, the snide remarks of the bystanders: 'Lucky man! Women should not be let loose!' These thoughts buzz around him like a swarm of angry bees.

'Will you be eating today?' His mother's sarcastic voice breaks into his troubling thoughts.

His appetite isn't affected, though. He eats well and has a royal nap.

When he wakes up at five in the evening, he is ushered into the real world by his mother. 'Oh! So you've woken up at last. Where are you off to now? A man who can't work or do business. And he's gone and got married. He can neither take care of his wife, nor can he control her! Stylish lady! Look at her clothes and her hair—worse than a whore! She twirls her husband round her little finger and makes him dance to her tune. Watch her in action when she comes home in the evening! For her, the husband is an empty coconut and I, her sasumai, I am not her mother-in-law, I am cow dung!'

'Shut up!' Peter screams.

'You can only tell *me* to shut up. Do you dare to say it to *her*, you coward? A real man would have slapped her and put her in her place. But you... I pray to the Lord to have pity on me and take me away soon, to free me from all this!'

Peter does not wait to hear any more of the usual litany. Rolling out his bike, he pedals hard in the direction of Caetan's taverna. An animated round of tablam-khell is going on in the verandah. Accompanied by, 'Ee-ree-ree-ree!' the long bamboo dice are flung to the ground. The atmosphere is spirited and lively. Ordering a four-anna tot of feni, Peter takes his glass and joins the spectators.

'Eight!'

'Twelve!'

'*Tabl*... That's it!'

'Congratulations! That was good!'

The players move away, as do the spectators. Everybody talks at the same time.

Peter has begun to unwind a little in the relaxed, noisy atmosphere of the pub. Just then, Agnel claps his hands and, when he has everybody's attention, he announces, 'Listen, who was there at the station this morning as the Vasco train was pulling out?'

'I was there!' Martin exclaims.

'Good! Anyone else?' Agnel continues. Peter is wary. Agnel's malicious tongue could be targeting him.

'Listen! Our dear Bab-Peter's beloved wife Bai-Teresa would have fallen under the train today!'

'W-h-a-t?' the crowd exclaims.

'But she was very fortunate. Bai-Teresa's gallant friend was travelling in the same compartment, just waiting for her, perhaps! Like a Hindi-movie hero, he bravely clamped his hand under her arm and pulled her into the train. Like this!' Agnel enacted the scene for the audience with a flourish that infuriated Peter.

'Mind your tongue, Agnel!' warns Peter.

'Am I exaggerating? Okay then, you tell it!' Agnel sniggers.

'You won't get away with this!' Peter shouts.

'So! What will you do? Come out in front if you must yap!' taunts Agnel as he pulls him forward.

Unable to back his empty bluster, Peter stays put.

'What a tough guy! Flaunt those muscles to your wife, if you have the guts!' Agnel rubs more salt into his wounds to the accompaniment of guffawing laughter.

I have to take all this because of that Teresa! Everyone disrespects me because of her! In the morning at the station; all those taunts! Guilherme's father's lecture! Mother's jeers! And now this! I'm not going to remain quiet!

Peter downs another tot—an eight-anna one this time.

The evening train announces its arrival with a piercing toot just as Peter cycles his usual way to the station. As Teresa gets down, Peter glances up sharply towards the compartment. He spots the hero of the morning sitting at the window. As she sits on the cross-bar of the cycle, Peter feels that Teresa is positively glowing this evening. He senses his bile rising.

'Pedru, you know, I was so scared this morning! If he hadn't pulled me in, God knows what would have happened!' Teresa relates, blissfully unaware of Peter's darkening countenance. Or the artery that is pulsing wildly on his forehead. Or that his eyes have become bloodshot.

The cycle comes to a stop at their house. Both get down.

'Pedru, tomorrow we'll leave earlier! I don't want to go through this…'

Before she can even comprehend what's happening, both of Teresa's cheeks turn crimson as Peter's slaps fall on them. She shrieks in pain while her mother-in-law calmly takes in the scene from inside. Encouraged, Peter goes berserk, and pummels her cheeks, her nose, her back, her stomach, her hands, her face…

For Death Does Not Come

It is high noon. The sun, like a ruthless foe, is literally branding her body. Below, the baked earth, and above, the unrelenting orb of fire. The whole body is engulfed in heat, like a pie being baked in an oven. The all-encompassing heat is unbearable.

The month of May is long gone and June is almost at an end. There is no sign of the monsoon. The earth is scorching hot. Thirsting, she looks beseechingly towards the sky, but there is not even a hint of a cloud to be seen. She turns her gaze tearfully away but not a single drop squeezes out of her eye.

The mango, jackfruit, banyan and coconut trees have all pitifully withered away and have shed almost all their leaves. The few that remain are scorched. They live only because death does not come. If this is the state of big trees, what about the grass and the shrubs? The grass has long since disappeared and arid sand has taken its place. And shrubs? Only pitiful dried sticks stand as a reminder.

The fields have merged into the plains. Wells have dried up, one after another. Lakes and tanks have become parched. Even the mud has cracked up into hard boulders.

Human beings have abandoned their homes and gone far away and the birds have all migrated to other lands. Cattle have perished. Whatever life is still surviving is marking time for death.

In this terrible noonday heat, the water-snake is hurrying along with her young one. How can anyone travel at this time? And, of all beings, a snake who has to rub her entire length against the earth for locomotion! Her body must be aflame. But the water-snake does not seem to be aware of it. Shepherding her young one along, she keeps moving on. Anybody watching her would surely call her mad. But...who is there to watch?

Through fields and plains and over dykes she hurries. Reaching a coconut tree, she pauses a while in its shade. She lets out a sigh, gathers her child and resumes her trek. She herself doesn't know where she's going.

They come across a field. God, how vast it is! But there is no time to ponder and the ground is too hot to tarry. Descending from the bund, she moves along the ridges. Oh, Mother! Anybody watching the water-snake would surely pity her and ask, 'Water-snake dear, why do you travel in this harsh, noonday heat? Will you reach the other side? You may lose your life! Retrace your steps and come back to this bund. Take shelter in the shade of this great banyan tree till evening.' But the water-snake would not have listened. At the most, she might have replied as she slithered on, 'Who has the time to rest? And so what if I die on my way? I live only because death does not...'

The ridges of this field are crumbling. She can only feel

the sand against her body. The sand: hot, blazing! The snake remembers the time when she had entered the house of Jose, the gram-merchant, in pursuit of a rat. From a corner, she had seen an open, concave earthen vessel containing sand kept on a blazing fire. When the sand was well heated up, Jose had put the gram into it, and then... She trembled with the sensation that moving over this hot sand, she felt like that gram that was being roasted!

My! The water-snake heaves a sigh. She can see a bund in the distance and, on the edge of it, a tree! It will afford her some shade for some time. Quickening her pace, she reaches the dyke. With an effort, she climbs onto the bund and glides into the shade of the tree. Where is he? Where's her baby? He was here only now! A great fear seizes her; she hurries back along the bund and looks... The baby is down. Thinking that the young one could not climb the bund, the snake leaps down it. What? Why is he so still? She touches the young one and...

With a sorrowful heart, the snake climbs back on to the bund and rests under the tree. She begins to reflect on the past. One incident after another comes to her mind.

As long as the father of her baby was around, she didn't have to bother about anything. He would see to all her needs. And how he doted on their children! One day, he had gone out in search of food when he had become very thirsty. Entering a thatched outhouse, he had seen a vessel of water. Anticipating a long cool drink, he had put his head into the pot. Suddenly, a merciless man had struck him on the back with a stout stick and had broken his backbone. Somehow, he'd managed to escape and shuffle his way back home. They had made every effort to save him, but...

At that time, the water-snake had felt that she, too, should die... What was the point of living? But no! Before dying, her mate had told her to take good care of the children and bring them up well. Yes, she had thought, I have to live for the sake of the children. But fate was very cruel!

The summer had ended yet, the rains, which should have come, did not. All the wells dried up and the lakes became parched; not a drop of water could be had, even for medicinal purposes. Through these difficult times, she managed to look after her children. She went hungry so that the children would not be deprived. But when the earth itself had no water, what could she do? One child died of thirst and just the two of them were left. Mother and child. The entire village became empty. The cobras, the great rat-snakes, and all the others had left. They were the only two who had remained behind. The water-snake had stayed on, hoping that the rains would eventually come. It was only when it became impossible to stay back that she had decided to move. Abandoning her burrow, she had gathered her child and set out... And now, that child, too, had abandoned her! Two more tears dropped.

'Why do you weep, water-snake?' a kind voice suddenly asks. The voice reminds her of her husband. Another couple of tears squeezes out of her eyes. 'Please don't cry!' the voice implores.

The snake looks around in wonder but can see nobody on the bund. Leaving aside the lone bibo tree, there isn't even another plant around. Can it be the bibo, then?

'Yes, it is I, the bibo, speaking. Why do you cry, my dear?'

She looks up at the tree with tear-filled eyes. She feels as if the burden of grief has eased a little. Sighing heavily, she narrates all that has befallen her. He was saddened by her tale, but what could he do? He only sighs and remains silent.

The snake asked, 'You are all alone here! Aren't you fed up?'

'What can I do? Earlier, vines would creep up on me and bushes would grow by my side. Along the edge was a coconut sapling too. But... But now, I am alone here, counting my days. When I remember that young sapling, I feel pain! He had not even begun to bear nuts. He's gone, poor fellow!'

'Don't take it amiss because I ask, Sir. What makes you live on?' inquires the snake.

After a long pause, the tree replies, 'There's nothing left in my life now. I know that sooner rather than later, I shall die. I live on, dear water-snake... I live only because death does not come!'

The tree lives on because death does not come! Do I, too, live on for the same reason? No! I was living because of my children, but who do I have now? Why should I live?

'I know what you are thinking, dear. Listen to me.

There are many living beings in the world. Many are disillusioned and frustrated. A large number, having fulfilled their duties, are free of their obligations. But they do not think of their death. They wait patiently for the time of death decreed by fate. You shouldn't die. Listen to me. About seven or eight miles east of this place is a small lake. Go and stay there. Nobody else knows of it and I don't think anybody else will reach there. Go now. You have to strive to live on until death comes.'

The water-snake looks up at the great tree as she readies to leave. Her eyes begin to well up.

'Could you do me a favour, please?'

'Tell me, Sir. Your wish is my command. Should I stay here?'

'No, dear. If you remain here, you will not live. You have to go. But before you go, do something for me...' The tree's voice was wavering. 'It has been more than a month since any living being has come near me. Please run over me freely and let me feel your touch. Just this once!'

The water-snake slithers over his shoulders and walks on his arms. Forgetting her own grief, she frolics and skips about on the tree. Eventually, she gets down. The tree is content.

With one last look at her dead child and a poignant farewell to the tree, the snake turns her head east and starts on her trek.

The same pitiless sun burns down. Though it is late afternoon, the earth is still hot. The sun is tilting westwards and soon it is evening. The sun begins to set; it disappears below the horizon, but its dying rays streak across the sky. The earth, which at this time generally looks like a radiant bride, today seems like a feeble invalid on her sick-bed. Eyeing this transformation in the environment with distress, the water-snake moves forward. Sunset turns to dusk and soon it is night and, then, dawn. The water-snake is drowsy, but she cannot afford to sleep. What if she falls into a deep slumber there? She has to reach that lake first.

Yet another noon! Again the searing heat! The water-snake crawls onward, tenaciously. Noon turns to evening. What is that? How is it possible? On all sides, the trees have withered, and are standing like bare poles. In their midst, however, are plants with bright green foliage! Staring at the sight in amazement, the water-snake surges forward.

Yes, this is the lake! And these plants are thriving because they are on its banks. So I have reached it at last! Wonderful! This water is so limpid! The water-snake stands there for some moments admiring the sight. Snapping out of her trance, she steps forward. She comes to the edge of the water. Before she touches her thirsty tongue to the water, she remembers her mate. He had died just when he was quenching his thirst! She remembers her children. They had died thirsting for water. And the bibo tree who is shrivelling for want of water and lives on only because death hasn't yet come.

It is now dark. Night comes on with gentle steps. The

water-snake enters the lake. She's seeing water for the first
time in many days! She drinks to her heart's content. She
prances and capers about. She feels drowsy and then falls
asleep.

The sound of splashing water wakes her at dawn.
Wondering who could be splashing water at this early
hour, she raises her head to find humans milling about!
She lowers her head quickly in fright.

She cautiously raises her head once more. She had
once seen water being pumped out of a lake into a nearby
field. Now she sees water from this lake being pumped
into a tanker. Damn these human beings. God alone knows
how they came to know of the existence of this isolated
lake? Now they will suck up every drop of this pristine
water and take it away. Nothing will be left... And then...

The water level falls... The lake is soon reduced to
half... Very soon there is very little water remaining.

'Hey look! A snake!' someone shouts. 'Get me a stick!
Hurry up!'

The snake shuts her eyes in resignation. Briefly, she
recalls her mate. She is gratified that she will die in the
same way that he did. She spares a fleeting thought for her
dead children—thank heavens they died before her. And
she remembers that bibo tree who had sent her here. He
must be still standing there on the bund waiting for death—
a death that has not yet come!

'A-a-a-h!'

'Good shot! It took just one stroke!'

Happy Birthday

'Hello! This is Amod, Amod Desai. Is Fernandes there? I mean Kevin Fernandes.'

'Hello Mr Desai, Mrs Fernandes here. Kevin has just gone to the grounds with Baba for football practice. The selections are just round the corner, no? Any message?'

Kevin works in the Accounts Section. Whenever they meet—even for official work—Kevin keeps talking about his son. About how smart he is and how well he plays. He was saying only yesterday that if he was selected for the state junior football team, he would go to Punjab with the squad next month. Fernandes had probably even used influence to try and get his son selected. Mrs Fernandes, too, never misses an opportunity to praise her son. Why else would she tell him that he'd gone for football practice?

'Do you have any message for him, Mr Desai?'

'Oh yes. Not only for him, but for you too. Chaitanya, I mean my son, is celebrating his birthday the day after tomorrow—that would be Saturday. We're having a small party at home in the evening. Both of you, I mean all three of you, should come over. I've phoned to invite you.'

'Saturday? Baba's practice ends between six-thirty or seven. You know, the selections...'

'No problem, Mrs Fernandes. It doesn't matter if it's late, but do come. I'm counting on you.'

As he hung up, Amod glanced at the football he'd brought for Chaitanya. He'd hoped that it would excite some interest in the game in his son. Only this morning, Harsha had taken it from the top of the cupboard, dusted it, and placed it on the floor. Stifling his urge to kick the ball hard, Amod had gently tapped it under the sofa.

'No striker can kick the ball better or harder than my son! If the keeper attempts to stop it, he's bound to land inside the net along with the ball!' Fernandes had once said. After Fernandes had left, Gauns, the peon, had wryly commented, 'This Fernandes pampers his son no end. I wouldn't be surprised if his son kicks him some day!'

'Did you get Fernandes?' Harsha asked in-between calls on the cellphone to her friends.

'No. I got his wife. She's no better!'

'Why? What happened?'

'Nothing other than bragging about Baba?'

'Baba?'

'Her son. It seems he's busy with pre-selection football practice. There are lots of good players and not all are selected. I've heard that Kevin has even put in a word with the minister. If his son is selected, I bet Kevin will report sick at the office and accompany his son to Punjab.'

Chaitanya has no interest in any game. When they bought the ball, he'd broken three glasses and a window pane within two days.

'Hi Indira! I've been trying your number for so long.'

'How did I not see your missed calls?'

'I was trying your landline. I forgot what a happy wanderer you are and only now thought of calling you on your mobile. Where are you?'

'She must have gone to the park. Taking her kids there is just an excuse for her to show off!' remarked Amod.

Upset with Amod's comments, Harsha covered the handset with her palm and said to him in a muted but incensed voice, 'You talk so loudly! Do you want her to hear? Keep quiet now.' Returning to the conversation, she said, 'Amod was just talking to Chaitanya. Once Amod is home, his son will just not leave him. He doesn't even want me. What's that noise, Indira? I can hear kids screaming. Are you at the park? I guessed as much.'

'Why don't you join us with Chaitanya? The garden is beautiful now and the kids are enjoying themselves!'

'I do feel like coming, but just can't seem to find the time. Besides, I don't drive, nor do I have a scooter like you do. I have to depend on Amod, and you know his sense of time—he doesn't get back before dark. After that, who wants to go?'

'Come right away! There, Gauravi's come with her two kids—you have only one to look after. I haven't seen him for quite some time; you hardly ever take him out. Just come. He'll get a chance to play, too. Tell Amod to drop you—it isn't far.'

I wonder how sincere her coaxing is, mused Harsha as she answered, 'You know, Indira, Chaitanya isn't too fond of going out—and he just doesn't like the park. Today,

wonder of wonders, Amod came home early. He wants to
play with Chaitanya. There he goes, playing football with
him. No, no… Right here in the house.'

It was time for Chaitanya's feed. Amod picked him up
and plonked him on to the chair by the dining table.

'Amod, please feed him, I've kept his Horlicks ready…
Sorry Indira, I was talking to Amod. Chaitanya's so
stubborn. We have to cajole him into eating. Amod, at
least…'

'By the way, why did you call?' Indira must have been
in a hurry.

'Gosh! I kept talking of everything else. I'd phoned to
invite you for the birthday. Yes, Chaitanya's—the day
after tomorrow, on Saturday. Come around seven in the
evening with the kids and your husband.'

'Sure! Which hall?'

Indira had celebrated even her child's fourth birthday
in a hall. Of late, this had become a fashionable trend.
Besides, there's music, dancing, games, magic shows and
tricks—adults enjoy themselves even more than the kids!

'Why in a hall? Our flat isn't cramped. Besides, we have
the open terrace. You've seen it, haven't you? We've
enclosed it now because of Chaitanya's antics. There he
goes again—I get worried. No, we aren't inviting many
people. Only the ones closest to us. And tell your hubby
please.'

Switching the handset off, Harsha quipped, 'Ever since
she's thrown a party in a hall, Indira feels that everyone
else, too, should do the same!'

Mopping up the Horlicks which Chaitanya had spilt, Amod remarked, 'Why shouldn't she celebrate in posh hotels? Her husband's working for the Food and Drugs Administration. The hotels eat out of his hands and the catering, too, is on the house. That's what people say!'

'I guess so. Last year, she had gold bangles made for her daughter. Of one and a half libra or so. She was proudly flaunting them. I hope she doesn't envy the chain which we made for Chaitanya now.'

'Why did you have to invite Indira? I'd told you not to call her. The way she preens irritates me. And that husband of hers, too, thinks no end of himself just because he's a government officer. I haven't forgotten what happened when we went for the birthday party!'

'What was that?'

'Don't you remember? He was most concerned about why we hadn't yet enrolled Chaitanya in KG?'

'In fact, I had told Indira that we didn't have much faith in KG or Montessori. I'd quoted what our famous poet Manohar Rai Sardesai had said, "KG means Kilogramme— a heavy weight on the tiny brain of a small child!" When I said it, she laughed as if I had cracked a joke.'

'I, too, had told her husband the same thing and that a child should not be admitted to school before the age of six. I'd said that we would teach him all those nursery rhymes and games at home. But the guy has a distrusting nature. He asked me, "Does your child have any problem?" I was so irritated!'

'Perhaps Mrs Amonkar told them. Indira knows her quite well.'

'I don't think so. Mrs Amonkar seems to be a pretty decent person. Don't you remember how, when we couldn't get him into pre-primary school, she'd put in a word and we'd been given admission on a priority basis?'

'But then, she herself called us and told us that the other children were getting distracted. They would stop their work to look at Chaitanya!'

'But what she said was for our own good. She told us that some of the rowdy kids were teasing him and...'

'Then we should have been concerned. But why did she have to say that other parents were complaining?'

'That's not what she said. She said that it was better if we admitted him to another school before other parents complained. In fact, she herself advised: "Chaitanya is not happy in school. He's a bit different from other children. People will begin to talk all manner of things about him. Rather than that..."'

'Didn't she tell us that there were schools for special children? And that if we wished, she would put in a word for admission to one named Daddy's Home? The bottom line is that she, too, felt that Chaitanya was abnormal, right?'

'But her intentions were good. She recommended the film *Taare Zameen Par*!'

They had gone to see the Aamir Khan-starrer only because Mrs Amonkar had told them to. Poor Ishaan's plight had moved them to tears. They were angry at the behaviour of his parents. When they returned home after the picture, Chaitanya was in deep sleep. He looked so sweet! Harsha had remarked, 'We, too, should have got a teacher like Ram Nikumbh!'

After seeing the picture, Amod had brought a colouring book and a large box of crayons for Chaitanya. But it didn't get Chaitanya interested. In fact, one fine day, in his hunger, he had even chewed up a couple of crayons.

'Mrs Amonkar is very understanding. She loves children. She's so nice even to Chaitanya. If ever she opens a school, I'd gladly entrust Chaitanya in her care.'

'Okay, okay. You seem determined to invite Mrs Amonkar. Go ahead. But then she'll ask how Bunty is. What do we tell her? That we've given her away to a friend?'

'Um, got it! We'll ask Cyril a favour and borrow Bunty for a day. We can tie her far away from Babu.'

Harsha's eyes gleamed. 'Great idea! Of late, keeping a Pomerean has become fashionable. It enhances the beauty of a flat, it seems!'

'How many times have I told you not to say Pomerian just because others say it? Use the right name: Pomeranian,' said Amod, dialling a number.

Mrs Amonkar's Pom had littered last November. She'd given a pup to Harsha saying, 'This is Bunty. Children love pets. If Chaitanya takes to him, he'll make him a good companion to play with.'

On the very first day, Chaitanya had grabbed a handful of Bunty's snow-white fur and just wouldn't let go. At first, the pup yelped several times and then bit and scratched the child. The biting and the scratching stopped only when Chaitanya yanked the tuft of fur right out of him. That same night, Amod gave the pup away to Cyril.

'Nobody seems to be taking the call at Mrs Amonkar's. Do you have her mobile number?'

'No, I don't. We can try later in the night. Meanwhile, call Dr Kerkar.'

Dr Kerkar, a paediatrician attached to the Maternity Home, had been called when Chaitanya was born. Amod was pleasantly surprised to find that he was an old schoolmate. He had earned a reputation as a capable doctor besides being a very good writer.

'Congratulations to both of you, you have a healthy child!'

They'd happily distributed three kilos of peddas. As he was popping the pedda into his mouth, Dr Kerkar had toasted them, 'Harsha and Amod mean happiness without bounds. And the child that has come into being is evidence of that 'chaitanya'—liveliness!'

Amod had seized upon the word 'chaitanya' for his child's name. He had made it a point to invite Dr Kerkar for the barso, the twelfth day mandated for the naming ceremony. From then on, Kerkar had become a family friend.

Even after a month, Babu couldn't lift his head even briefly. 'Some babies take some time to hold their heads up.' Dr Kerkar's calming advice seemed to be borne out when Chaitanya began to hold his head up at three-and-a-half months. But it took him six months to turn over. The neighbours made their anxiety worse.

'What? He hasn't begun to crawl yet?'

'Look at the eyes! He blinks all the time.'

'He is pale rather than fair.'

'He has good looks but there's something a little odd about him.'

Can all babies be uniform? Even all our fingers are not the same. But then, we can't keep people from commenting either.

Harsha stopped inviting friends over, but the baby's birthday was celebrated. There was excellent food followed by scrumptious ice cream. Babu cried at the beginning of the party but fell silent afterwards. He finally went to sleep.

Babu hadn't learned to walk even at one. Aaji, his grandmother, commented, 'My Amod began to walk after fifteen months. It must be hereditary.'

Dr Kerkar who had come for the birthday party, later took Amod aside and remarked, 'Do you find Chaitanya normal?'

'Why, Doctor? His progress is a little slow, that's all.'

'I suspect cretinism.'

'What's that? What did you say?'

'No, nothing. But if you find that this slow progress continues, come and see me. We'll run a few tests on him.'

In fact, Chaitanya's progress was slower than that of other children. He would remain silent for hours. Sometimes, he would laugh for no apparent reason. But when anybody tried to make him smile, he wouldn't. He cried when he was hungry. Unlike most other children, Chaitanya never kept them awake at nights. He would drool continuously. But then, so did some other babies. He couldn't communicate when he wanted to relieve himself. But again...

'My mum says that I used to soil the bed till I was five. Perhaps he got it from me,' Harsha tried to rationalize.

But when Harsha's mother pronounced that she was worried, Amod took Chaitanya to Dr Kerkar.

'It's true that Chaitanya's development is slow. It isn't as if we are really worried. But since you'd mentioned it, I've come. Examine him, and decide whether he has a problem and if it is genetic or otherwise.'

After examining Chaitanya, Dr Kerkar said, 'I wouldn't be worried just because his physical growth is slow, but wait, Amod, we'll get an EEG done first.'

They got an electroencephalogram done. Things seemed okay, except that...

'Brain growth is not what it should be. That is the problem.'

More tests followed, after which Dr Kerkar's initial fears were confirmed—cretinism due to neo-natal thyroid hormone deficiency.

Harsha was on the verge of sobbing, 'Why did fate have this in store for us, Doctor?'

'He'll be cured, won't he, Doctor?'

'We'll give him some medications to improve the hormones. But don't expect miracles. He will grow up as a cretin child. You have to learn to live with that. You will have to handle him as his needs dictate...'

'For how long? How many years?'

Dr Kerkar said nothing. He wrote out a prescription and handed it over to them.

'Come tomorrow morning, I will show you someone.'

They didn't understand what Dr Kerkar meant till they went with him the next day to see a patient of his.

'See him.'

They saw a boy standing in the corner of the room. A cot was placed along the middle of the wall. On the other side a cupboard was placed angularly, to form a cubicle to confine the boy. The child, about two-and-a-half feet in height, was looking at them blankly. The clothes the child wore seemed more pleasant than the child who wore them—the open mouth, the drooling saliva, and the large popping eyes—they couldn't take it!

'Guess his age. He is twenty-two years old.'

They found it difficult to believe. They'd seen dwarfs, but he didn't look like one.

'How is this possible?' Harsha blurted out.

But Amod was looking at the boy's lips. He could see a few tufts of hair sprouting there. He couldn't say a word.

He finally mumbled, 'Our Chaitanya...?'

'No. This is a case of microcephaly. It is a congenital abnormality. The skull does not expand, so the brain cannot grow. Eventually, the growth of both the brain and the body is stunted.'

'What is the future of such a child, Kerkar?'

'His body will be okay, but the brain will remain underdeveloped. Most of his faculties are at a standstill.

We've found his IQ to be sixteen. He won't grow any more.'

'What about his parents?' Harsha asked in a tremulous voice.

'They hope against hope that, eventually, the child will smile at them and talk to them, but it won't happen.'

When they were out, Dr Kerkar asked them, 'Don't you think that what fate has wished on you is at least better than this? Yours is a cretin child. He isn't a child with microcephaly.'

'Won't Chaitanya be cured, Dr Kerkar?'

'That depends on what you mean by cured. If you mean, will he study, play or sing, you can't hope for that. But lavish him with understanding and try to make him happy. His parenting will be your challenge...'

And both of them had accepted this challenge.

'What happened? Can't you get through to the doctor?'

'I had been getting an engaged tone for quite some time now. But the minute you spoke, it's started ringing.' Amod turned to Dr Kerkar, 'Hello, hello Dr Kerkar, Amod here, Amod Desai.'

'Hello, Amod! How are you? And how is our Chaitanya?'

'He's okay.'

'Did he get violent again?'

'No. Meaning not too much. Once...' His voice trailed off because they hadn't decided whether to tell him about the time when Chaitanya had grabbed and pulled Harsha's hair.

'It's good to see that you treat him with so much love, Amod. Okay, so what did you phone about?'

'Dr Kerkar, we're having a party for Chaitanya's birthday.'

The doctor was quiet for a moment. What could he be thinking?

Chaitanya's first birthday had been celebrated on a grand scale. The second had been a very private affair. Just during the days of his third birthday, they were in the Sutak. The mourning period for a distant uncle served as an excuse to skip celebrations.

Just before his fourth birthday, Chaitanya became unwell. He had diarrhoea and vomiting. Dr Kerkar advised them to take precautions so that he would not be exposed to any infection or contagion as, 'you know that his level of resistance is low.'

This last year had been good for Chaitanya, except for....

'That's great, Amod! Go ahead.'

Envisaging Dr Kerkar's beaming face, Amod extended the invitation.

'You *have* to come, Dr Kerkar. We haven't invited many people—only those closest to us!'

'Sure! When did you say it was?'

'Saturday. The day after tomorrow, around seven in the evening—at home.'

'Okay, I'll be there. Except if there's an emergency...'

'Of course. But do come even if you're late.' Yes, before Dr Kerkar can put down the phone, he must ask him something.

'Can I ask you something, Dr Kerkar?'

'Of course! What's that?'

'We think that Baba will behave well. But then again, we can't be certain can we? Meaning—if—in case he... You remember, last time, you'd given him a syrup to sedate him. Tomorrow—I mean—on Saturday—there'll be people—I mean, could we give him something?'

Once, when he'd brought some work home from office, Chaitanya had urinated on some important papers. In his anger, Amod had instinctively slapped him. The racket that Chaitanya had unleashed had been unbelievable! Nothing would stop him. Screaming away, he had lifted a small stool and flung it at his father. Then, he wouldn't allow anybody to approach him. He calmed down only when Dr Kerkar was called and a syrup was forcibly administered to sedate him.

When Dr Kerkar did not immediately respond, Amod hurriedly added, 'Not that we will necessarily give it him. In fact we won't. But...'

'If you find it most necessary, you may give him Largactil syrup.'

'Thank you, Doc,' said Amod, distinctly relieved.

'What did the doctor say?' Harsha wanted to know even before he had cradled the receiver.

'He said we could give it. Tomorrow, when you go to the chemist to buy diapers, get a bottle of Largactil paediatric syrup.'

'Good! I'm done now. I've finished all the calls I was supposed to. Try Mrs Amonkar one more time.'

The call went through immediately.

As soon as she got the invitation, Mrs Amonkar responded warmly, 'Sure! I'll be there to greet Chaitanya on his birthday. How is he? Does he enjoy playing with Bunty?'

'Yes, of course. He plays.'

'Our doggy has littered again—four pups this time. Should I get Chaitanya one more as a birthday present?'

'No, no. One is enough. And please don't bring a present. But do come.'

As he put the phone down, he remembered and dialled.

'Hello, Cyril. Desai here. Do me a favour. On Saturday evening around six, I'll be coming to your place. Lend me Bunty for one night. I'll return her on Sunday morning. Okay? Please. Thank you!'

Harsha lifted Chaitanya on to her lap and laid him across it. Taking a small pair of scissors, she ran a hand through his hair and snipped off the knots. Pacifying the squirming child, she soothingly told him, 'We're going to celebrate your fifth birthday in style! There, there, that's my smart boy! Remain still, whatever anyone may say.' Harsha gently trimmed his beautiful, curly locks. 'Other kids start screaming the minute you touch them, but not my Babu. My pet is really smart!'

Setting the scissors aside, she propped Chaitanya on the sofa.

'So everything done, Amod? Are there any arrangements left?'

'I've confirmed the catering order. Mallya is the only

one left to be invited. He hasn't got a landline yet, and I don't have his cell number. Tomorrow, before going to office, I will go over to his place and invite him. With that we'll be done with the invitations.'

Running her fingers through her son's hair again, Harsha remarked, 'Babu seems to have improved a lot, hasn't he? He drools much less. He seems to have grown taller too, no? Tomorrow in his new clothes, he will definitely look like a prince. Then, everyone will realize that he isn't as abnormal as they thought!'

The next morning, when Amod rang the bell of his flat, Mallya had sat for a pooja. Over his protests Mallya's wife brought him tea. Just as he was admiring their brand new rented apartment, the middle-aged Mallya entered, pulling on his shirt.

'How are you Mr Desai?' Mallya greeting him warmly in his lilting Mangalorean Konkani.

'I've come to invite you for my son's birthday. On Saturday evening. All of you must come.'

'Wah, wah! Very happy news!'

Suddenly, with a dismayed cry, Mrs Mallya emerged from inside. 'Just see what your son has done, he has messed up everything!'

Mallya rushed inside and, the next moment, Amod's ears were assaulted with the loud smack of a slap and the high-pitched howling of a child. Wondering what had happened, Amod peeked inside and found that Mallya Junior had scribbled to his heart's content on the newly painted walls. If it was an ownership flat, it would be another matter. Realizing that the landlord of the rented flat would certainly not be amused with this scrawling on his new walls, the senior Mallya was tapping his forehead in anguish. Amod made a diplomatic retreat.

When he reached the office, he related the incident to Gauns.

'You know something, boss? A child's scribbles enhance the beauty of a home. Those who have an eye for it, will see the art in it. For those who don't, it is mere scribbling.'

Amod recalled Mallya Junior's scribbles and tried to imagine some art in it. Could those be clouds in the sky? Or perhaps a forest of trees? Or was it the scattered fur of a Pomeranian?

He returned home in an upbeat mood. Harsha was waiting for him eagerly. Chaitanya sat blinking in front of the TV, which was on, in the hall.

'I've brought the diapers and the syrup to sedate him too. Tell you what, we'll give him the syrup before seven. He'll be yawning by the time the people start coming. Afterwards, we'll put him to bed. And he looks really sweet when he's asleep! Nobody can make out anything. In fact, when he smiles in his sleep, he looks so good that we almost have to worry about him attracting an evil eye!'

'Excellent idea! We'll put him to bed here in the hall. And listen, tomorrow morning, get all his toys. The football, the model cars, the soft toys…'

'Yes, I'll do that. I'll arrange them all neatly.'

'No, no! Don't arrange them neatly. Scatter them around carelessly. A child's home has to look like one.' And, taking out a pencil from his pocket, he began to scribble happily on the wall behind Chaitanya.

'Everyone should know how much Chaitanya plays...how he scribbles on the wall...how naughty he is...'

Electoral Empowerment

Durga dozed off, waiting for Ratnu to return. Tomorrow was election day. Since Ratnu had taken upon himself the task of providing breakfast and lunch to the party workers, Durga had already boiled and readied the potatoes. She had wanted to go to bed early so as to be up at dawn for the long day ahead. But here she was, yet to reach her bed.

She was rudely shaken awake by Ratnu who had returned home past eleven, bellowing, 'Why haven't you peeled the potatoes? Get up! Peel them and then go to sleep!'

Realizing that Ratnu had had quite a few drinks, Durga decided that she had no alternative. Splashing cold water to drive away the sleep from her eyes, she got on with the job.

Early to bed and late to rise was her idea of pleasure. Unfortunately, she wasn't fated to attain this dream. Ever since her marriage, Durga had never been able to do what she wished. She had always done what Ratnu had wanted her to do.

As her fingers mechanically peeled the potatoes, her mind slipped into a reverie. It was soon after she had been married. She had made a curry of jackfruit nuts; just the way her mother did. To her dismay, Ratnu was very irritated by it. Gripping her by the hair, he had warned her, 'Remember this, you will cook what I like—not what you or your people like!'

From that day onwards, Durga had suppressed all her likes.

Having finished peeling the pile of potatoes, she decided that she might as well chop them into cubes. By now she had lost her desire for sleep. Ratnu, however, was already snoring as usual.

Durga's elder brother, too, had the habit of snoring as soon as he went to bed. But, after his marriage, his habit had changed. He still snored, but well after going to bed.

Thoughts of her home brought a lump to her throat. Her hands stopped working. Yes, it had been four long years since she had been home to see her parents. She'd gone just once since she'd been married. There had been one more time when she had set out to go...

Her mother-in-law had brandished a stick of firewood, threatening to hit her. Grabbing whatever clothes she could, a terribly hurt Durga had rushed out of the house, determined to go back to her parents. But as she was waiting for the bus, Ratnu had arrived, seized her by the arm, and dragged her back home. He had threatened her, 'Don't you dare step out of this house again! You will never go anywhere without my permission!'

That sealed the doors of her parental home for her.

Covering the cubed potatoes, Durga got up, washed

her hands, and, wiping them on her the pallu of her sari, finally went to bed.

Four years ago, she had entered this house as an enthusiastic bride. Which wide-eyed bride does not feel that her husband's house should be greater than her parents' house? Durga was happy, but her happiness did not last long. Wealth is not necessarily synonymous with nobility of character. Instead of being esteemed for being educated, Durga was only mocked at by her illiterate in-laws.

One day, she poured out her emotions into a letter and gave it to her neighbour, Ranga, to give to her brother. God knows how, but that too, reached Ratnu's hands and, God! how furious Ratnu had become! That day, the mark of five fingers had bloomed on Durga's cheeks. Ratnu had issued a final diktat. 'Let me warn you just one more time: if you try to do anything behind my back, I'll flay the hide off you. Don't think that you can do anything without my coming to know of it!'

Durga had resolved that, henceforth, she would only do what Ratnu wanted her to. She no longer had the courage to do otherwise.

She felt too lethargic to get up early the next morning. But, today, laziness was the one thing she could not afford. Today was Election Day.

Ratnu was strutting around like a host. Actually, Vassu was only a distant relative but, as soon as he'd announced his candidature, Ratnu had promoted him to second cousin. He had taken upon himself the job of campaign manager.

Tramping from house to house, Ratnu had sought votes for Vassu. Vans were despatched to advertise meetings, banners were strung up and posters pasted. Ratnu had performed his task with vigour. He handled the catering, including the all-important liquor.

Ratnu was positive that Vassu would win. Durga was certain that if Vassu won, Ratnu would go around claiming that Vassu was his first cousin!

By seven-thirty in the morning, workers had started coming in for breakfast. By nine there was a long queue. At ten there was some respite. Just then, Ratnu came in with Vassu. As she was serving them, Durga's ears caught snatches of their conversation.

'Are the vehicles going around properly?' asked Vassu.

'Of course! I'm keeping an eye on them personally. The people from the upper ward have almost finished voting. The tempos are fetching voters from the lower ward now.'

'You needn't have sent the vans there. I doubt those people will vote for me. I wouldn't put it past them to ride in our vehicles and vote for my opponent!'

'Forget it! They wouldn't dare!' Ratnu twirled his moustache menacingly.

'How does one know who voted for whom?' Vassu asked, his forehead creasing.

'Bring the tea in quickly!' shouted Ratnu from the door. Durga scampered to obey.

Past midday, three batches of a dozen workers each had been served food.

Durga was tired. But she gulped down a couple of mouthfuls of rice and went off to wash the utensils. She then went to lie down for a much-needed rest.

Ratnu came in and shouted, 'What are you lying there for? Don't you know that it's Election Day? Get up! Go and vote!'

Durga got up. She knew that people were supposed to vote. But she hadn't realized that she, too, could vote. Unbidden, a thrill passed through her body. A hitherto unknown enthusiasm gripped her. She dressed, went out, and asked Ratnu, 'What do I do when I get there?'

'How dumb can you get!' Ratnu fumed. Then, with exaggerated patience, he explained, 'Show them this card. They will call out your name and give you a paper and a stamp. Look here. This is Vassu's symbol and his name. You have to stamp the space next to it. Understood?'

Durga nodded. Despite this, Ratnu repeated the instructions several times. 'Stamp the ballot paper properly! Don't stamp in any other place. Do just as I tell you.'

Saying, 'Okay,' Durga set off.

She went to the polling station and stood in queue. Ratnu's words rang in her ears, 'Do just as I tell you!' What else had she been doing all these years? Had she made jackfruit seed curry? Had she visited her parents? Had she written to her brother?

Do as I tell you, he tells me. As if I have the guts to do otherwise!

Durga's name was called out. 'Ratnu's wife,' someone whispered. An election staffer marked her finger with indelible ink. Another handed her the ballot paper. A third placed the stamp in her hands. A polling booth had been fashioned with a curtain in a corner. To ensure that no one else would know whom one had voted for, she guessed.

So that no one should know?

Absolutely no one?

Durga remembered Vassu's words: 'How does one know who voted for whom?'

Durga who, till now, had only done what Ratnu had told her to, suddenly grew taut.

She strode to the cubicle. Unfolding the ballot paper, she searched for Vassu's name and symbol. She covered it with her finger and promptly stamped all the other symbols. Calmly folding the ballot paper, she dropped it into the box.

Smiling triumphantly, Durga turned homewards.

Sand Castles

I wake up to find the darkness of the night lifting. A new day.

Every Sunday morning, the amplified sound of Mass being celebrated in the nearby chapel wafts over to my ears and sets me thinking, O God, for keeping me alive this day, may God bless you.

The very idea of God blessing God makes me smile. When I was a medical student, our professor of cardiology had had a sudden heart attack and died in the middle of a busy schedule. Even I was surprised. It didn't seem right that a doctor should die in that way...When a patient goes to a doctor and finds the doctor himself down with fever, won't his faith in the doctor suffer?

True, a doctor, too, is human. But, drifting away in sleep at a ripe old age, with a hint of a smile on his lips, is the sort of death that befits a doctor.

All very true. But then, you could also have an ill-fated doctor like me. Why did this rare demon, Osteogenic Sarcoma, have to haunt *me*?

'Are you awake?' Shami arrives, and asks.

Stifling a sigh, I simulate a yawn.

'What a lousy show by India!' Shami's remark reminds me that the Test match has begun today. The radio commentary was to start at five-thirty in the morning. To avoid any last-minute hassles, Shami had bought new cells for the transistor—because of me!

'What's the score?' I feign enthusiasm.

'India's batting. Gavaskar has gone for a duck. The score hasn't even touched hundred, and five wickets are down!'

'Daddy, Kapil Dev's come out to bat. Let's see now!' This nine-year-old Ajay is even crazier than me about cricket. And Kapil Dev is his idol.

'Thank God I didn't wake up early!' I say with a laugh.

'I called out to you earlier, but there was no response, so I thought I'd let you sleep on,' says Shami.

How would I wake up? I fell asleep only at one-thirty or so in the morning. I wonder if Shami is aware of it. Was she, too, awake and feigning sleep like I was?

'Getting up, aren't you? By the time you have a wash, the tea will be ready.' Shami goes into the kitchen.

These days everyone is so solicitous about me. Shami, of course, is my wife. She should be bothered. But even sixth and seventh cousins are overly concerned.

As I throw back the covers and prepare to get up, I am held back by Munni's little arm round my neck. This child has the habit of sleeping with her arm around her Daddy! I gently unravel her arm. Yes, one by one, these ties will have to be loosened.

I wash, and sit down for a cup of tea. The stereo is

playing one of my favourite cassettes: Bismillah Khan. Whenever the distinctive notes of Bismillah's shehnai hit my ears, a thrill of expectation goes through my body. But today the tune sounds heavy with distress. I know that the distress is in my own heart. The refrain from my heart as it mingles with the notes of the flute causes this! How can the plaintive Bhairavi from my heart match the lively Lalit from the shehnai?

But Shami must not know. Her endeavour is to make me happy. As I usually do, I keep time by drumming on the table with my fingers... This time, for Shami's sake.

Shami finishes drinking her tea. I reach out for my cup to finish mine. Inadvertently, my hand knocks it over. Shami hurries over and mops up the spilt tea.

'Shall I get you some more?'

'No, thanks.'

Shami drained her cup. Why did mine spill halfway through?

No doubt, all of us have to die some day. Everyone knows this. But no one sits and counts his days. We do not put off today's work for tomorrow because tomorrow we may not be around. We all know that. But has that ever prevented anyone from postponing things? Nobody has stopped accumulating wealth for tomorrow. Tomorrow and yet another tomorrow will dawn. And then another...countless tomorrows.

For me though, the story is different. That monster dreaded by the whole world, and known as the Big C, has picked me out for his special ministrations.

I now have very few tomorrows left. I have to stop putting things off.

But why? If I won't be around tomorrow, why should I even bother about today's work?

'Aroo, shall we go to Mangeshi Temple tomorrow?' Shami asks.

I feel like smiling. Since when has Shami become religious? Shami, who normally raises her voice against all forms of ritualistic religion…

'Stop laughing now. Please! And don't ask me why?'

But I keep a straight face and agree. Shami has a faraway look in her eyes and, by way of explanation, she quotes a Konkani saying: 'A lost person's mind seeks here, there, and everywhere!'

'Shami, you are not lost! There is Ajay. And Munni. You just cannot get lost. Sweetheart, life is such. Do you know how many people die suddenly in accidents, without any warning to their families?'

'I'm not interested in that!' Shami's voice is choking with emotion.

'I, too, don't know the exact statistics, but we should consider ourselves more fortunate than those people… Now, now, Shami, no tears please! My dear, don't be foolish. How often have I told you…'

'Aroo, don't! I'm not strong like you! But I'll try and be brave.'

'That's my girl!' I say, patting her hair.

Shami is normally what we Goans call 'straight-backed'. She will not bend before any pressure. But sometimes she behaves oddly. The other day, all of a sudden, she resigned from her treasured job as a higher secondary lecturer without even telling me.

I clearly remember the day a fortnight ago. I'd asked her why she hadn't gone to college. She had replied matter-of-factly, 'I've given up my job.'

I had been stunned! 'Have you gone mad, Shami? You could have asked me at least!'

'Would you have agreed?'

'Of course not! And what will you do now that you are jobless?'

'I will stay at home.'

'Idiot! Had you not worked all these years, it wouldn't have mattered. But you've resigned *now*! When you most need a job!'

'Today I have no need for a job. *Today* I need to stay at home,' Shami had replied very calmly.

'Maybe not today. But tomorrow! You are only thinking of today. Think of the future. Think of the children.'

'Just don't bother your head, Aroo! I have thought over everything carefully. It's a lecturer's post. I can get a job whenever I want to.'

Shami is normally very analytical and wise. But stubborn to a fault.

'Daddy, Daddy, eight wickets down!' Ajay is totally immersed in the commentary.

'Turn off that commentary! It soured half my mood as I was getting up and, now, it will spoil the remaining half.'

In fact, during Test matches, I used to even play hooky

from my hospital duties to catch the commentary. Knowing this, Shami had put new cells into the transistor and has kept it ready for my sake. But of what use is a dish full of delicious morsels if one has no appetite?

I take up the paper and sit down to read the news. But I can't concentrate. I browse through it as usual. Mechanically scanning the headlines, the editorial and the sports news, my glance stops at the cinema ads.

My eyes begin to quiver. *Anand* is playing. I'd seen the film about five or seven years ago and liked it a lot. With death staring him in the face, Anand, the protagonist, spends his remaining days bringing happiness to others.

Today, I have myself become Anand.

I must see the movie today. When I'd seen it that time, I'd enjoyed it. I wonder if I will this time? Yes, I must see it! I call out to Shami. Unbidden, the anxiety in my heart has found its way into my voice. I call out again.

Shami comes running. 'What's happened?'

Her consternation amuses me.

'My! How scared you look!' I laugh.

Shami is on the verge of tears. 'Enough of your jokes! Why did you call out?'

'Shami, shall we go to the cinema today?'

Shami, who normally jumps at the suggestion, becomes alert at the word cinema. She looks into my eyes. Silent. Analysing.

'What film?' she asks apprehensively. She must know that *Anand* is showing!

'*Anand.*'

Shami is about to bite down on her lower lip. Knowing that my eyes are on her, she gives up the attempt.

She shakes her head and says with finality, 'No! Any other picture. Please don't insist. I won't be able to sit through it. And you… And you, too, cannot go.'

'Okay, Shami, drop it! It was just a suggestion. Forget it. And see, don't get all emotional. It's just not like you.'

Shami goes back inside without a word.

Shami's state weighs me down. I know what she's going through. I am truly fortunate and, mercifully, it has happened to me. Had it happened to Shami, I don't have to imagine what my state of mind would have been.

The doorbell rings.

Dr Bala Savaikar comes in. We were once classmates and Savaikar now lives in Mumbai.

'When did you come?' I ask.

'Just yesterday,' Savaikar replies.

And he lapses into silence.

All these people come to see me and sit dumbly, not knowing what to say. Their silence is killing. It is always I who have to ask some trite question to break the silence. But this time, I keep my mouth shut. I want to see how long this fellow will sit quiet!

Savaikar straightens himself at last and asks lamely, 'How are you?'

'Fine!' The usual response springs from my mouth.

Savaikar drifts into silence once again.

But I can't restrain myself now. I laugh as I say to him, 'Haven't you come to inquire about me? Go ahead, ask.'

Savaikar wonders if I'm being rude. He stares at me and then suddenly breaks into an easy laugh. 'You haven't changed, man!'

Turning serious once again, he says, 'I got the news in Mumbai. I didn't believe it... But, Arun, you've been foolish! You should have come to Mumbai. I'd even left a message at the Tata Memorial to let me know the minute you landed there.'

'Thanks! And forget it! I, too, want to forget it... I don't want to live as a patient.'

'Nobody becomes a patient by choice.'

'I know, I know! Had there even been the slightest glimmer of hope, I would have gone not only to Bombay but even to the States. But you know that it is Osteogenic Sarcoma...and...late stage!'

'That's what I heard. I felt wretched. But Arun, I'm surprised. How did it escape you?'

'Destiny! It was fated to happen. I felt a slight swelling in my back. Thinking that it was just a swelling, I asked Shami to massage it. I thought I felt better, so I did nothing more.'

'Then?'

'Last month I'd gone to Raikar's X-ray Clinic because of a patient. He had just installed a new screening machine. In jest I stood before the machine and asked him to screen me. Suddenly, the colour drained from his face. He was stunned! He immediately did an X-ray of my chest, processed it right in front of me, and confirmed it. Both lungs showed metastasis! I couldn't even imagine it... But it was too late!' Was I babbling?

'But, my dear man, why have you just resigned yourself to fate? There are so many new drugs. The frontiers of medical science have advanced so much! Were there things like chemotherapy twenty-five years ago? New therapies keep coming up. You ought to have taken a chance!'

'It's easy to tell that to a patient. It's not so easy to convince a doctor,' I say with a smile. 'Tell me frankly, had I come to Bombay would my cancer have been contained? I have mets in both lungs… What would they do? Surgery? Right? That too radical! Results? Temporary relief, if at all. Rather than that, it's better to end my days happily! Numbered though my days are, why should I spend them in misery?'

Savaikar has no answer.

Shami brings some tea.

'When did you come, Bala?'

'Just yesterday.'

Shami waits for him to continue.

But, without another word, Savaikar sips at his tea.

Shami goes inside. When she is out of earshot, Savaikar asks, 'Has she taken it very badly?'

'No!' I lie. 'I've given her a fair idea of everything. We are prepared to face whatever has to happen, boldly and cheerfully.'

Savaikar departs. I'm sure he won't help admiring me. The idea of meeting death face-to-face with a smile makes even me feel good. It boosts my mind to a philosophic plane!

Shami calls me for lunch as soon as she finishes frying

the bhajjas. Prawn bhajjas! These puffs of shrimp, fried in gram-flour batter are my favourites. Of late, Shami has been serving delicious new dishes, one after another, every day. Whatever I like, whatever I enjoy, she's been cooking for me.

I taste the bhajjas.

The fact is that I've lost my old appetite. I feel hunger, but there seems to be no connection between my stomach and my tongue. My tongue does not have its usual vitality... But I eat. To make Shami feel good.

'How are the bhajjas?' Shami asks.

'Excellent! One thing, though, Shami. You've been cooking lovely, tasty stuff for me every day. Now you must cook insipid dishes one day, salty the next, tasteless another. Make dal ros one day and bland curry the next. I'm fed up with such good tasty food every day!'

Shami laughs.

'Can I say one more thing?' I ask.

'What's that?' Shami asks, raising her eyebrows.

'Quarrel with me like before!'

Shami keeps silent.

Really, this illness has taken away the flavour from this house—no arguments, no differences of opinion, no heated discussions. Each one has taken it upon himself to keep me happy!

Ajay and Munni come running to me, 'Daddy! Let's go to the beach today!'

I glance at Shami. I'm ready to go if Shami wants to. Shami is ready if I want to go...

'Yes, let's go.'

Both the kids spring to life at my words. They run off.

Even I feel a thrill at the thought of going to the beach. We'll see if the free-blowing breeze from the sea will relax me more than the confined air of the house.

I lie down on the bed after lunch, but I cannot sleep a wink. Unknowingly, my hand travels to the lump in my back. The swelling seems the same, neither bigger, nor smaller.

Just a short time ago, I didn't even know of its existence. And now it has turned out to be Death's harbinger...

I've been fooled despite being a doctor. A post-graduate at that!

What great plans I had! I would go to America for a super-specialization in a couple of years. I would set up my own clinic on my return... Give Ajay and Munni a great education... And now? All had come to nothing!

What sacrifices I had to make to build up my career! All for nothing.

I always used to say that if a man manages to build a career and get a wife of his choice, he would want for nothing more in life.

But I forgot one thing—health! I forgot that, despite being a doctor.

And Shami! We fell in love and got married. No one opposed the marriage. Perhaps if somebody had opposed it, poor Shami would have been spared this predicament.

Ajay is a boy. He's the elder child, too. He'll grow up somehow. But I worry about Munni. She needs loving care. Because of my darling Munni, at least, I needed a few more years.

I've nearly finished paying the instalments on this flat. Within a year, it will be free from the mortgage. The balance can be paid off from my insurance money after I'm gone.

Everything I worked for—all for nothing. The name and fame that I earned! And all that I planned too, it's of no use… My head starts spinning with all these thoughts. I don't know how long I lose myself in my thoughts.

I start when Shami puts her hand on my forehead.

'Oh! It's you!'

'Whom did you expect?' Shami laughs. It sounds artificial.

'What's the time? Is it five?' I ask and hurriedly get up.

'It was five long ago. The kids are screaming to go.'

'Let's go then. Everybody out!'

Shami calls out to the children and tells them to put on their beach clothes.

I drink my tea, dress up and get the car out. By which time everyone is ready.

It's nearly six by the time we get to the beach.

Ajay has brought along a little bucket, a small spade and a plastic bowl to play with on the sand.

Munni is excited. The people on the beach, too, walk about with pleasant looks on their faces. The atmosphere is lively. My own, mood however, is glum. Even the breeze blowing in from the sea fails to lift my spirits. I just cannot concentrate on anything. Only a few days more and I'll never come here again... I just won't be around. This shore, this sun will be there, only... I'll be beyond the last horizon... This car, that flat, the fridge inside, the stereo, all these gadgets—I will leave all behind.

My Shami, my Ajay, my little Munni! They'll all be here. But I—only I...

I shake my head and move on.

Shami likes to sit in places where there are no crowds, no noise. We go far from the madding crowd and sit on the sand.

Ajay and Munni are at play on the sand. I cushion my head in Shami's lap and lie down. My gaze settles on Shami's face. Shami is looking towards the sea. How beautiful she looks! Her face competes with the flaming rays of the setting sun. Suddenly, my eyes alight on the kumkum in the middle of her forehead. This red kumkum will be her companion for only a few days more. Soon no kumkum will adorn her forehead...no, no! Before I depart, I must tell Shami. Give up those medieval customs! Don't give up your kumkum and advertise your widowhood. Wear it in my memory.

'Daddy! Ajay is not letting me play!' Munni comes crying to me.

'No, Daddy. She keeps destroying my house,' protests Ajay. I sit up and gather Munni to me. 'She's my smart little girl! Come, I'll build you a nice house.'

And I start packing the sand for Munni. Shami and helps us. Ajay abandons his game and starts gathering sand from around and dumps it near us. Shaping the wet sand, I begin to build a fort. Packing buckets with wet sand and upturning them, I raise the battlements. Neat majestic towers rise in the four corners. With the little spade, I sculpt the main gate. Pressing the plastic moulds of wet sand against the walls, I beautify them. And a truly beautiful fort is erected!

Shami gets up. 'Come on. Let's go now. Do you know the time? It's past seven.' It is indeed late. But Ajay and Munni are reluctant to leave. Even I hesitate.

We'd invested so much time, labour and love to build this sand castle. It seems so difficult to abandon it to the elements and just leave.

Shami gets irritated. 'Ajay, Munni! Will you guys get up? Otherwise I'll go home alone.'

I'm the first to stand up.

Ajay gathers up his bucket, spade and bowl.

'Are we supposed to leave this castle here and go?' queries Ajay tearfully.

Munni promptly replies, 'Of course! You're supposed to take back only the bucket and other things that you brought. The sand was always here. How can we take it? And so what that we built this castle? We have to leave it here and go. The people will all admire it and say, "What a beautiful castle!" Right, Daddy?'

I hug Munni tight. My little Munni, wise beyond her years, has dispelled the gloom that had shrouded my heart.

A Writer's Tale

I was in Delhi for a three-day literary seminar. Since I'd taken the evening flight from Mumbai, darkness had spread by the time I reached the guesthouse. The January cold bit into my body.

Collecting my key from the reception, I glanced at the register. Barring some seven or eight familiar names, I knew no one else. Most of the delegates hadn't yet arrived.

I ran into the Kannada writer K. Jalappa in the corridor. He greeted me with a handshake. 'Good evening, Sir. It's nice to meet you again.' Standing near him was a woman of about thirty in a kurta-churidhar and, by her side, was a stocky man aged sixty or so. 'Meet Ms Jayamamata. She's a Tamil writer,' Jalappa said by way of introduction.

'Hello, I'm Manohar,' I said, extending my hand before realizing that she had joined hers in a namaste. She hesitated momentarily but, before I could retract my hand, she thrust hers out. Her hand was cold to the touch. More than the low temperature of Delhi, I speculated that they were cold because she was nervous—daunted perhaps by the intellectual environment. When I looked questioningly towards the elderly, lungi-clad man by her side, she

explained, 'He's my uncle, J. Someshwaram.' He looked
at me with a blank face. When I put my hand out, he took
it without saying a word. I did not have to be told that he
knew neither English nor Hindi.

'Does he write, too?' I asked her.

'No. No. He's here as my chaperone'.

A chaperone for a woman her age? I found that strange.
But I kept my own counsel. As I was longing to relax, I
lifted my bag and, with, 'I'll be seeing you,' I turned
towards my room.

Rooms lined the corridor on both sides. As soon as I
entered 205, I switched on the heater. Gradually, the room
warmed up. Since I'd eaten in the plane, I wasn't hungry.
After reading for about an hour, I drifted off to sleep.

By the time I finished my morning walk, had a bath and
put on my clothes, it was past eight. I was going over the
paper that I had to present in the next session when the
doorbell rang.

'Mr Manohar?'

'Yes.'

'Time for breakfast. Shall we go?' said Jalappa who was
standing outside the door.

Behind him was the Tamil writer and her uncle.

'Good morning, Sir,' she greeted me.

'Good morning. Uh… I didn't quite catch your name.'

'Jayamamata,' Jalappa supplied the name, adding with
a smile, 'that is to say, Jaya and Mamata together.'

'Oh! I hope you won't give a tough time to the organizers!' I joked.

'Looking at her, one wouldn't say so. Because, leaving aside her name, there is nothing in common between the two dominant politicians of Tamil Nadu and West Bengal and our writer friend!' Jalappa said, perhaps attempting to take the sting out of our ribbing.

In fact, there was nothing remarkable about her. Her face was rather plain. Her looks lacked vitality and her cheeks were pimpled. She had a long neck and her hair was bundled in a bun. The bright pink sweater on a blue kurta-churidhar suggested an absolute lack of dress sense and colour combinations. When I'd seen her the previous day, I'd got the impression that she was rather dumb, but Jalappa's comments seemed to have roused her. As if she had suddenly found her voice, she said, 'Why not? They are passionate about their politics. I am passionate about my literary life'.

'That's good!' I said appreciatively.

The Tamil writer in her thirties, Jalappa in his forties, myself in the fifties and her uncle in his sixties—each of us representing four different decades—set out for the canteen. Suddenly, the uncle said something to her tersely. Jayamamata, who had just started to blossom, made a small face and, stepping out from behind him, went ahead.

'He's come to guard her, it seems,' Jalappa murmured.

Just then, I saw Giridhar Rai walking towards the cafetaria. I quickened my strides to meet my old friend. Chatting easily, we entered. I was surprised to see her having her breakfast alone.

Taking the seat opposite, I introduced her to Giridhar, 'Meet Jayamamata. She's a Tamil writer.'

'Call me Jayatha. Just Jayatha.'

'The name sounds beautiful!'

'It's my pen name.'

I then remembered. 'Where's your uncle?'

'There he is. Gorging himself.' She pointed.

I looked in the direction her finger indicated. Indeed, he was voraciously tucking into his breakfast.

'When he's eating, nothing can distract him,' she added. 'When we entered, he went straight to the only vacant place. I was relieved that I could sit here. When he finishes eating, he will come to escort me.'

Her dislike for her uncle was so patent that it was embarrassing even for the listener. Her unkind comments about her own uncle—nice though he may not have been—before virtual strangers, made me a trifle uncomfortable.

Jalappa entered the canteen. Spotting him, she drew his attention and invited him to sit in the vacant chair by her side. She was soon immersed in a discussion with him and I was occupied with my Hindi writer friend.

A coach was supposed to take us to India International Centre for the seminar. Basking in the tender rays of the winter sun, we chatted cheerfully as we waited for our transport.

Suddenly, a question addressed to Jayatha by somebody from the group reached my ears, 'Is it true that this is your first trip to Delhi? How do you like it?'

'I feel like a bird freed from a cage! My mind thirsts for a free environment. But...look over there. My uncle holds one end of the reins tied round my neck and does not allow me to fly. To ensure that my feet remain rooted to the ground, he keeps casting those watchful glances at me.'

From where I was, I looked curiously in that direction. Jalappa appeared a trifle uneasy. The others guffawed loudly. Uncle, probably blissfully unaware that he was the object of their collective derision, looked on impassively in silence.

The coach arrived. Jayatha was the first to enter it. Uncle was left behind. Jalappa went just ahead of me. Much like a sixteen-year-old calling out to her boyfriend, Jayatha said to him, gesticulating energetically, 'Come here! I've kept a place for you.' Throughout the ride, she prattled on endlessly.

When he got down at the IIC, Jalappa hurried to my side, 'I've been trying to get your attention, but this woman will not leave my side! I have a request for you.' Thrusting an envelope into my hands, he said, 'This is my new story, in translation. My friend has done the translation into Hindi. I want your opinion on both the story and the translation. Whenever you find the time, please go through it.'

Some time ago, when a story of his had appeared in *The Little Magazine*, I had given him a detailed critique which he had liked. I agreed to go through the story.

Jayatha then walked up and immediately wanted to know, 'What is that?'

Jalappa's forehead creased in irritation.

'Not for my ears? I see!' She pouted in disappointment.

'You don't have to know everything! C'mon, it's already late. Let's go,' Jalappa remarked, leading her in. Hard on her heels, her uncle followed in silence, tucking in his lungi.

The opening ceremony was very meaningful from a literary point of view. The keynote address was a little too lengthy but not boring. The seminar began after lunch. My paper was in the next session. The front rows were occupied by renowned and up-coming writer-delegates from all over the country. Despite a close look, I couldn't spot Jalappa. Making a mental note to read his story in my room that night, I concentrated on the proceedings of the seminar.

Jalappa's story was good. While the Hindi translation had a few minor flaws, the original in Kannada must surely be first rate. Just as I was putting it down after finishing it, the doorbell rang.

It was Jalappa. 'Sorry, Sir. Did I disturb you?'

'What is this, Jalappa? You know that I don't like being called "Sir"!'

'Sorry, Sir. I mean…sorry! I came to ask you. Shall we go for dinner together? What time do you wish to go?'

'They've mentioned that dinner will be served between

eight and nine-thirty. The mess is close by. We could go around nine. Is that okay with you?'

'It suits me fine,' he said, before adding hesitantly, 'I have a request. Please, come to my room about an hour before dinner.'

'Jalappa, I've just finished reading your beautiful story. It's very—'

'Sir… I mean Manohar… If you don't mind, we'll talk at length later. I'll just have a quick shower and get ready.'

'Instead, why don't you have a shower and come here?'

After hesitating a moment, Jalappa said, 'I have a bottle of Royal Challenge. I thought we could have a peg each before going for dinner.'

I'm not much of a whisky drinker, but I didn't have the heart to disappoint Jalappa.

'I'm in 208. Be there around eight,' said Jalappa as he hurried away.

At eight, I knocked at Jalappa's door. The next door opened. This door opposite mine was apparently Jayatha's. She was standing in the doorway and staring at me. I lifted my hand in greeting. Just then Jalappa opened his door.

Stepping forward, she said, 'If it's nothing private, may I join you?'

I was about to say, 'Please do,' when Jalappa hastily said, 'No. In fact, we want to talk in private.' Ushering me in, he shut the door.

'Why did you have to be so brusque with her?' Unwittingly, sympathy for her found its way into my words.

'No, Sir. You have no idea about the way she behaves. I now dread being near her. Do you know that she didn't allow me to listen to one single word at the seminar! And when you were reading your paper, she pestered me to take her out, saying that the strap of her sandal had snapped and that she had to buy new ones. Since she didn't know her way around, and didn't know Hindi, I took pity on her. She asked me to take her to Karol Bagh. After buying her sandals, I suggested we return, but she begged me to go with her to a fabric shop. After spending an hour there, she felt thirsty. As we were having juice, she ordered some snacks. When we finally got back, the day's proceedings had ended. To top it all, her uncle! As we were entering the IIC, he was standing there staring sternly at us. So embarrassing!'

'You don't have to get so worked up about it, Jalappa! She's come to Delhi for the first time. There's nothing wrong with her wanting to see the city. Try to understand her.'

But Jalappa was just not interested in talking about her. In silence, he poured out two pegs of whisky and unstoppered the flask of water.

The topic of the short story elicited enthusiasm from him though. From Jalappa's story, we moved to new trends in Kannada fiction, happenings in literature and the political games played by leading writers against each other. It was almost nine. So, saying, 'Shall we go to eat?' I got up. But Jalappa countered with, 'One for the road,' as he poured out a couple of half-pegs for us both.

By the time we entered the canteen, most people had already eaten. Uncle, who had just finished, was washing his hands, and Jayatha, too, had nearly finished her food. Jalappa deliberately chose a distant table. His act did not escape her notice. I felt that she was just lingering over the last few mouthfuls.

Jalappa was talking on as he ate, but my focus kept inadvertently shifting to her. Jalappa kept eating till she got up. We were the last to leave the canteen.

As we entered the corridor of the guesthouse we saw Jayatha.

'I was waiting for you. I have to make a trunk call home. Will you accompany me to the booth?' She was addressing us both, but it was obvious that she wanted Jalappa to go with her.

I was about to say to Jalappa, 'You go with her,' when he said, 'Why don't you take your uncle with you?'

'You know that I hate him. And he's gone off to his room. Do come with me, please!'

I felt sorry for her. 'Come on, Jalappa, let's keep her company. It isn't far.'

'Sorry, Sir. I'm too tired. You go. I'm going off to sleep.'

Glancing for an instant as he walked off, she came to me and said, 'Thank you, Sir!'

'Please don't call me Sir,' I said.

'But you are such a senior writer, how can I address you by name?'

'Rather than respecting the seniority bestowed by age,

you should honour the skill of the artist. I may be older than you but, nonetheless, just like you, I am a writer. I will be happy if you call me by my name.'

On the way to the phone booth, she asked her first question, 'Back there, what were you two talking about?'

'Nothing in particular. Mainly about his new story...'

'I know. You were talking about me.' She spoke in a hurt voice, but with a rather forceful tone.

'Please. Don't go barking up the wrong tree.' I thought of a valid explanation. 'You want to know the truth? We wanted to sit for a drink. How could we invite you there?'

For a brief moment, she hesitated. She couldn't make up her mind whether to believe me or not.

'You had a drink?'

'Yes. You don't believe me?'

'Open your mouth!' she ordered, and, childlike, I invited her to smell my breath. She came close and sniffed. A whiff of the strong perfume she had used entered my nostrils.

'I hate alcohol!' she pronounced.

'Who's asking *you* to drink?' I countered.

'I mean, I dislike people who drink.'

I was taken aback. When she realized the implication of her words, she immediately hastened to explain, 'I don't mean you. I like you.'

That left me even more confused.

'Not that I drink regularly. Whenever somebody wants company, I don't mind sitting with a glass. That's all.' I found myself furnishing an explanation.

She laughed. 'Do you know why I said that? My father drinks heavily. Then he talks all nonsense. I get irritated. But I suppose a drink is useful in this bitter cold, isn't it?'

Near the campus gate, Balraj, who was walking with Shubhada, greeted me, 'Hello, Manohar, night walk?'

'Yes. You're returning and I'm going—that's the only difference.'

'Well, enjoy your walk in youthful company,' he said, as he walked on with his sixty-year-old companion.

'The Punjabi writer seems to have become conscious of the Bengali author's age!'

I laughed at Jayatha's caustic comment and couldn't help admiring her sardonic wit.

As we walked, Jayatha seemed to be inching closer towards me. 'I'm shivering.'

The cold winter night of Delhi was made worse by a stiff wind that was blowing.

'Do you mind if I hold your hand for a while, Manohar?' Jayatha asked, and, without even waiting for a reply, she promptly grabbed my hand.

Her hand was cold to the touch. Rubbing it briskly with both my hands, I generated some warmth.

'Thank you, Manohar. That felt very good,' she said, but did not retract her hand.

'I have a daughter as old as you.' Why did I say that?

She immediately swivelled round to fix me with an unblinking stare, 'So what?' Once again I was confused. By this time we had reached the STD booth. She dialled home and kept talking for a long time. I was watching her bill mounting. When it reached ninety rupees, I tried to bring it to her notice by pointing towards the meter. But she talked on and on. I, too, phoned home and spoke with my wife. My bill came to sixteen rupees, while hers was a hundred and twenty-six rupees.

'I'm not bothered about the bill. My husband is rolling in money,' she said on the way back.

'What does your husband do?' Normally, I don't pry into other writers' private lives. But here, Jayatha was herself eager to exhibit hers. Her husband was a builder. Besides, her father-in-law ran a hardware business. They had a bungalow and several cars. Of her two children, one was studying at an exclusive public school in Ooty, while the younger was still in kindergarten. They lived together with her in-laws. It was a very orthodox family. Neither her parents' family nor her in-laws had the least interest in literary matters. Her own parents had never shown any appreciation of their daughter's achievements as a writer. Neither did her father and mother-in-law nor her husband praise her work as an artiste. In fact, her parents-in-law did not want her to write, but her husband felt that as long as her writing did not interfere with her domestic duties and provided it did not trouble anyone else, she could continue to write.

Thus, she would begin her day with her morning chores, after which she would send her daughter to school and cook the noon meal. After all this, Jayatha would make the time to write.

'My house is a prison to me. I live only because I have a pen and paper.'

'Could I get to read your stories? Have you brought any with you?' My curiosity had been aroused.

'Yes, I have some. But how will you read them? They are in Tamil. They haven't been translated into English or Hindi yet.'

'Could you relate any of your stories to me?' I asked.

'My English is not so good and I do not know Hindi.'

'No problem. Tell it as well as you can.'

'Now?'

'Now.'

'Which one should I tell?'

'Any one that you like.'

And Jayatha prepared to start her story. We sat on a bench in the corridor of the guesthouse. It was past ten-thirty at night when she haltingly began.

'The original story is in the first person. Should I narrate it that way?'

'Okay.'

'When I was little, my father gave me a doll. I really loved her. I used to always take her to bed with me. I grew up. With puberty came some restrictions. After high school, I was told to stay at home. Since I didn't have any friends to play and talk with, I became a loner. And one day it dawned on me that my doll was actually a boy. Of my own age. At first I became shy, but later I began to hug him and talk to him. It gave me great pleasure. At night I slept with him. I started feeling very safe with him around. One day, a little girl from the neighbourhood asked for the doll to play with. My mother was about to give my doll to her. But I became very angry.

'"You're too big to play with dolls now. Give it to her."

'"He is mine. Nobody else has any right over him."

'Mother raised her eyebrows in surprise, "What do you mean by *he* is mine. She's just a doll!"

'I felt as if I'd been caught. But I covered up, "Call it a he or a she—but I don't like to share my things with others," and, grabbing the doll, I went inside.

'That night, he was so happy that he hugged me very tight.

'My maternal aunt lived in a village some forty miles away. She had no children. She used to lavish a lot of love on me. I, too, liked her very much. One day, she came to see us and said to my mother, "I've not been keeping too well of late. I also feel lonely. Could you send your daughter to stay with us till you fix up her marriage? It would make me very happy."

'Mother asked Father. He too agreed to send me. Nobody asked *me* though.

'Nevertheless, I refused.

'"Soon you'll be married. Won't you have to go to your husband's house equally far away? You may as well get used to it," Mother said.

'It wasn't that I did not want to stay at my aunt's house. I did not want to leave my doll behind. I tried to take him. I even stuffed him into my bag. But Mother took him out, saying, "People will laugh at you!"

'I reasoned that I probably wouldn't get to take him to bed at Aunt's place. I hid him in my cupboard between my sarees and went to my aunt's house.

'Aunty doted on me. She gave me whatever I asked for. She would take me for long walks. My youthful body was filling out. Aunty would circle my head with dry chillies and salt, clockwise and anti-clockwise, to ward off the evil eye.

'One night, in that rustic dwelling of my aunt's, I could not sleep. I really missed my doll. Since my bladder was full, I opened the rear door to relieve myself in the bathroom outside. As I returned, I lingered at the door. The garden was bathed in the soft light of the moon and a gentle breeze was blowing. I was enjoying the pleasant atmosphere. Suddenly, a hand descended on my shoulder. It was my uncle. He caught me up in a hug and, before I could realize what was happening, he violated me. Against my will. Even though I cried. Hearing me cry, Aunty reached the scene. Uncle hurriedly got up and went back inside. I was still sobbing. Aunty herself lifted me up, straightened out my clothes, and took me inside. Uncle was trying to explain—he claimed that I called him out and... But Aunty had understood everything. The next day, she consoled me and asked for forgiveness. She also told me not to tell anybody. She then immediately brought me back to my parents' house.

'I was disgusted. But despite that, I knew how to conduct myself. I behaved as if nothing had happened. The first thing I did was to put my hand in my cupboard. But "he" wasn't there! I panicked. Could Mother have given him away? When I asked her, she told me that she had dumped him in the loft. I desperately ransacked the entire loft and finally found the doll under some old clothes. I brought him into my room and shut the door. And, how amazing, the doll had turned into a girl! A pubescent girl with globes sprouting on her chest. She smiled at me. I was tense. But, after a moment, I relaxed. How could I have confided my predicament to "him"? It would certainly be easier to tell "her". I could now unburden my heart to her.

'She was soiled, so I took her to the bathroom. I saw blood on her. She was menstruating! I hugged her tight and began to sob. Wiping away my tears, she said, "Hush, dear. We womenfolk cannot escape this."'

Jayatha paused. I was listening very attentively. This garrulous and seeming simpleton of a woman—and such a beautiful story! I was dumbstruck.

'You didn't like it, did you? I didn't tell it properly. The original in Tamil is quite good.'

'Jayatha, the story is very beautiful. The original must be superb. Great! Hats off to you. I would like to hear more of your stories. But it is late now. Let's go back.'

From where we were seated I saw that Jalappa had opened his door and come out. Seeing us on the bench, he went back to his room and shut the door. In fact, Jalappa should have been here. After listening to the story, he would have probably revised his opinion about Jayatha, I thought. Deciding to tell him about it tomorrow, I got up.

Almost reluctantly, Jayatha, too, stood up. 'Manohar, if you don't mind, shall we take a walk?'

'Are you crazy, Jayatha? Just see, even in here, you're shivering with the cold!'

'If you are with me, I will not be bothered about the cold.'

This was just too much!

With finality I told her, 'Sorry, it is very late. If you want, you may join me at six when I take my morning walk.'

'No, Sir. I am a late riser,' she said as she turned towards her room. Stopping for a moment, she turned back and extended a hand towards me, 'Thank you, Manohar, for your attention, and good night.'

The next morning, I had just returned from my morning walk when the bell rang. Balancing two cups of tea in his hands, Jalappa entered. Taking one of the cups, I said, 'Great way to begin the day with a cup of tea! Thanks, Jalappa.'

'You're welcome.' And, as if he couldn't wait to get it off his mind, he said, 'She was talking pretty late last night, wasn't she? How did you find her?'

'Excellent!' I said, referring to the story.

'You mean you weren't bored stiff?'

'Not at all! Jalappa, have you read any of her stories?'

'No.'

'You should judge a writer by his writings. Not by his or her behaviour.'

'But, Sir, do you know that she is a psychiatric case? She's okay only because she's on medication. As for me, I'm very apprehensive about her, lest she lands me in some scandal!'

'Who told you she had mental problems?' I asked, intrigued.

'Who else? She herself told me.'

'So, instead of praising her for her frankness, is it right for you to castigate her? The fact that she is aware of her problem and can talk about it is praiseworthy.'

But Jalappa wasn't ready to buy my explanation. Mumbling, 'She'll make others mad!' he went on his way. I couldn't help wondering if she had perhaps made advances towards Jalappa.

Exchanging 'good mornings' with other delegates, I arrived at the cafeteria. Jayatha and her uncle were sitting there face-to-face, discussing some obviously serious matter. Finding a table near the periphery, I sat there. As I was buttering my toast, Jalappa walked in.

'Good morning, Sir—I mean, Manohar. I thought Jayatha wouldn't leave you this morning!'

'Why? I'm not young and dashing like you!' I said, taking a bite from the toast.

'For her, anybody will do!' Jalappa remarked instantly. Realizing the implication of his words, he tried to make amends. 'Sorry, Sir. When I said "anybody", I didn't mean you, Sir. She's such a pest. Everybody else gives her a wide berth. As soon as she arrived, she caught hold of Sharma. Then she tried me. Now...'

'Now she's edging towards me, right?'

'I'm not saying that. But she...'

'Look here, Jalappa, I don't like being judgemental about others. I regard her as a fellow writer.'

'Of course, Sir. But if she herself starts talking about her private life unasked, what does one do? And what does one do when she behaves intimately, as if she were one's girlfriend?'

I replied, 'How will she tell somebody who's not ready to listen? After a couple of attempts, she will obviously abandon the effort. As for me, I'm ready to listen. I'm prepared to empathize with her... I may even find a character for a story!'

I sat in the coach that would take us to the seminar. Jayatha, too, boarded it.

'Good morning, Manohar,' she greeted me and sat next to me. Uncle, who got in just behind her, proceeded to sit on the last seat by himself. Jalappa entered the coach and, seeing us together, smirked, as if to convey, See! I guessed this would happen.

'Is Jalappa angry with me?'

'Why ask me? Ask him,' I said.

'I feel very light today. As if a great burden has been lifted off me. Do you know why?'

'No. Why?'

In fact, I was not interested in the drift of the conversation, but I didn't want to be rude.

'Uncle is a very greedy man. He is actually my husband's uncle. He has squandered his estate with his vices, and survives now on the charity of my father-in-law and husband. He has been sent to keep an eye on me. You know, this is the first time that I have got out of the house. Before this, even when I received the State Award, they didn't allow me to go receive it. This time, it was only after I convinced them about what a prestigious seminar this was, did they allow me to come. That, too, with a condition: "Only this time! We won't send you anywhere else." They've sent me here under these stringent conditions. With this old man! He's been given twenty thousand rupees for expenses.'

'And nothing's been given to you?' I asked.

'My husband's given me twenty thousand rupees. He's told me to buy whatever I want. Uncle has to account for the twenty thousand rupees which my father-in-law gave him.

'We don't have to pay anything for the rooms here. He's proposed that if I report that we paid room charges at the rate of a thousand rupees per day for each of the two rooms, I would be free to go wherever I wanted and do whatever I wished. I agreed to the deal. Which is why he is sitting quietly behind us—see!'

I was astonished by the unethical agreement, but said nothing.

At the seminar, too, she continued her prattling, disturbing me and other delegates. On the pretext of going out for a glass of water, I took a different seat when I returned.

After lunch, Jayatha sought me out again. She said, 'Manohar, will you please come with me!'

'Where to?'

'To Karol Bagh. The sandals I bought yesterday are hurting me. They promised to exchange them. Please come with me!' Jayatha implored, holding on to the sleeve of my jacket.

I plucked her hand from my sleeve, and told her firmly, 'Look here, Jayatha. I've come here to attend the seminar. I won't leave it and wander around. If you want, you may go.'

Looking disappointed, Jayatha went off.

That evening, as we were streaming out of the hall after the final session, Jayatha stepped out of an autorickshaw. Balraj was talking excitedly about the outstanding paper that Mitra had just read, while Sushruti was suggesting ways in which it could have been even better.

'Hello, Manohar! I managed to go and come by myself!' Jayatha announced proudly, as if she had achieved a great victory. I wasn't pleased by the way she had butted in. In fact, no one approved of her.

'So, what did you buy?' Mitra asked.

'Sandals. The price was six hundred rupees. I managed to beat them down to five hundred, so I bought two pairs!' she remarked enthusiastically, displaying the sandals.

With a little haggling, they could have been bought for a hundred and fifty rupees. Though everyone realized this, nobody said anything.

'Don't you like them?' she asked me.

'You're going to wear them. You have to like them,' I said, noncommittal.

When we entered the coach, I found a vacant place next to Vikram. I like to talk to as many writers as possible at such literary gatherings. I was still in conversation with Vikram when she entered. She pouted, then sat behind us.

She may have felt slighted, having presumed that I was avoiding her. But her anger did not seem to last long. As we were alighting from the coach, she hurried over to me.

'Manohar, do you have any water?'

'No. If you were thirsty, you should have drunk water in the conference hall.'

'I clean forgot about it. I need to take my medicine. Please come with me to the mess.'

'Okay. But where's your uncle today? I haven't seen him since morning.'

'God knows! Since he's managed to make his money now, he must be sleeping in his room.' And, quickly changing the subject, she said heatedly, 'I went to Karol Bagh all by myself. You didn't even bother to ask me about it!'

'Sorry. So, how did you go?'

'I took an auto.'

'By yourself? In the first place, you don't know a word of Hindi. Why did you take the risk of going alone in a strange autorickshaw?'

'Then, why did you turn me down?' she shot back. The next moment, she was excited once more. 'But the driver was a nice man. He did everything that I asked. He came with me to exchange the sandals. Then I took him with me to buy a bottle of perfume and a couple of bras. Since I don't know Hindi, having him with me was a great help.'

I was flabbergasted to say the least. It was possible that she had gone shopping for lingerie with Jalappa, too. That would account for his irritation!

'We roamed around for almost three-and-a-half hours. Do you know how much he charged me?'

'How much?'

'He asked for sixty rupees. I gave him a hundred and fifty. He was really a nice man! He didn't take any advantage of me.'

'And if he had?' I asked irritably.

'I don't know! I had to go alone because you refused to come with me.'

At the cafeteria, she washed her medicine down with water. On the way back, she asked, 'Do you know what that tablet is?'

'How am I supposed to know?'

'You just don't have the habit of asking! I feel nice when people, especially friends, show concern.'

'Okay. So I'm asking—what tablet is it?'

'I'm undergoing psychiatric treatment.' She paused, expecting a question from me, then continued, 'Two years ago, my younger sister died. I was very fond of her. She was very loving.'

'What happened to her?'

'She had come down with pneumonia. She died within eight days. I was shocked. I went into a depression. I even had to be hospitalized. I'm still on medication.'

'I'm sorry to hear it. But, Jayatha, don't brood about it too much. It's part of life. One has to accept it. You can't just fold up. In any case, your sister won't come back. Because of your parents at least, you have to be strong,' I said, wondering if there was any truth to her story.

'It's because of them that I suffered a breakdown! We observe a remembrance ceremony for the dead after a month. Relatives and close friends are called. After the religious rites, everyone sits for a sumptuous meal. On that day I lost my head. Mother was busy cooking. Nobody had time to grieve. And Father? Father was closeted in the room dyeing his grey hair! I told him, "Appa, at least today, when we are observing a remembrance for the dead, couldn't we dispense with this make-up!" And do you know what he said? "How can I meet our relatives looking like an old man? You must go inside and dress properly, too." Appa seemed to be pleased to meet our relations. He was humming a tune! I couldn't take it any more. I rushed to the kitchen and grabbed a knife. Appa was only saved because I was restrained by family members, otherwise...'

Jayatha's breathing had quickened. Unknowingly, I caught her hand, 'Calm down, Jayatha. Such people do exist in this world. Isn't it because we come across such persons that we become writers?'

'You know, Manohar, I have written a story on this very subject. I wrote it just as it came to me and the story became very famous. The publisher specially wrote to me praising it.'

'What about your father? How did he react after reading it?'

'Nobody at home ever reads my stories. The only one who used to read them was my sister. And, she's dead. Now I don't have a single friend.'

I sensed a tremor in her voice.

'But, Jayatha, you have your husband, your dearest friend...'

'No. He is not my friend. He is only my husband.' Her tone had suddenly become hard. 'Yes, I have everything. I have a house. I have a husband and I have children. I have loads of money. I can buy anything I want. But... But I don't have a friend.'

My heart filled with sympathy for Jayatha. When I'd looked at her as a writer earlier, I had been amazed. My literary instincts were really impressed by her talent. And now, when I saw this new side to her, I was surprised. To put it more accurately, I was dazed. How could one label her? A simpleton? A flirt? A creative person? An emotional woman? Or just plain mixed-up?

We had almost reached the guesthouse. Her uncle was looking at us from the doorway of his room. But she didn't look at him. I wanted to leave, but she stood rooted to the spot. In a voice that had turned thick with emotion, she asked, 'Manohar, will you be my friend?'

There was hope in her eyes.

I said, 'Of course, I will! Bye for now,' and turned to go. But she hadn't finished. As if announcing it to the whole world, she exclaimed, 'I'm so happy today! Thank you so much!'

I glanced around nervously, but I needn't have worried. Barring her uncle, who was standing mutely in the distance, there was nobody around. I unlocked my room and entered it.

Tomorrow was the last day of the seminar. I was on the panel of the morning study session. Brushing up on the subject, I made my preparations for it by noting down a few points. Exactly at eight-forty-five in the evening, I got up for dinner. When I opened my door, I found Jayatha sprawled in a chair that she'd placed across her open door. Seeing me, she quickly got up. Pushing the chair back inside, she locked her room and dashed across to me.

'Where's your uncle?'

'He had come to take me to dinner. Just then, I saw Vikram so I told Uncle to go along with him and that I would be coming with you.'

We had just crossed the corridor when she suddenly stood still. Then, whirling towards me, she remarked exasperatedly, 'You are absolutely unobservant! Tell me, how do I look?'

I took a step back and looked. Jayatha was wearing a tight pair of slacks and a sleeveless top which had a plunging, revealing neckline. To start with, Jayatha had a very plain face. Her cheeks were sunken and pimpled. Her collar-bones protruded below her thin neck. Neither was her figure anything to write home about. And with these clothes, to me at least, she appeared positively ugly.

'So, how do I look?' She preened before me.

'You want my honest opinion?'

She may have detected the flat tone in my voice, because she said in a deflated voice, 'Tell me the truth.'

'I would not have approved of my daughter wearing such clothes.'

'And your wife?'

'My wife would certainly never have worn them!'

'Many men, who don't like their wives to wear such clothes, enjoy seeing other people's wives in them.'

'Jayatha, I don't want to get into this. It's very cold outside. You won't be able to stand the cold in these clothes.' Realizing that she would then launch into 'as long as you are with me' nonsense, I added, 'If you want to come with me, you had better go back inside and wear a long-sleeved sweater. Bring a shawl along, too.'

Jayatha went in quietly. She emerged wearing a sweater and carrying a shawl. As we walked along, she edged closer.

'You know, Manohar, I really like the way you order me about.'

I mentally slapped my forehead in exasperation.

As we reached the mess, Jayatha's uncle was leaving, belching in satisfaction. 'You eat and come. I'll wait for you here,' he told her.

'No! Don't wait for me. I have to make a phone call after dinner. Manohar here will accompany me.'

I did not understand the Tamil they spoke, but their body language was so obvious that I was pretty sure that this was what they said. What followed this, though, was beyond my comprehension. The conversation flowed like a rapid, staccato round of bursting firecrackers followed by a welcome pause, after which Uncle walked out while we entered the mess.

I sat where Jalappa was eating, along with Jayatha.

Beyond curtly acknowledging her presence, he didn't utter a word to her.

'I've waited only to hear your panel discussion. But I have to catch the twelve-thirty afternoon flight. Which means that I'm not sure that I'll be able to stay till the end,' Jalappa told me.

'If you happen to be in Goa, do come over,' I said.

'Of course, I will. But, before that, my collection of short stories is being released in Bangalore soon. You will receive the invitation. I will be happy if you can make it.'

'I will make it a point to come,' I replied.

'It looks like I won't be invited.' Jayatha just had to open her mouth.

Nonplussed for a moment, Jalappa countered with, 'Will you come if I invite you? I thought you said that you are never allowed to go out.'

'That's also true,' Jayatha said with a crestfallen face and began to eat.

Jalappa finished his dinner hurriedly and got up. 'See you in the morning,' he said.

I wonder if he even finished eating properly! The thought came to me, but the words emerged from Jayatha's mouth, who looked at me and laughed.

We finished our meal and went out. The cold, coupled with the stiff breeze, was biting. Jayatha's teeth had begun to chatter. I said, 'Come on, I'm longing to get inside the room and sit in front of the heater.'

Making a face, Jayatha asked, 'Shall we go and make that phone call?'

In fact, in this bitter cold, when it was unthinkable to even sit inside a room with the door open, walking along the open road was nothing short of penance. But I didn't feel like hurting Jayatha. The other reason was that my writer's instinct was aroused and I wanted to know more about her. We began to walk towards the phone booth.

'Did you find the story I related yesterday, vulgar?'

'Not at all! In fact, I liked it very much.'

'Many people who read it asked me how the story came to me! But I've never told anybody the truth. But...'

'But what?'

'I thought that you would ask whether such a thing had occurred in my life.'

'Okay, then. I'll ask you now. Tell me.'

'Yes. I, too, had a doll... It is actually my own story!' She held my hand tight for no apparent reason.

'How many stories have you written so far?' I asked.

'Many! You know, I'm fascinated by man–woman relationships. And then I write just as it comes to me. Some people praise my writing, but most accuse me of crossing the limits of morality. When women write about sex they have to adhere to the mores of society, it seems. Do you feel the same, Manohar?'

'Definitely not! A writer need only be true to his art. Be it violence or sex. Who says that only men may write erotic stuff?'

'Thank you!' she said as she released my hand and caught hold of my arm.

'Manohar, there is a novel growing in my head. It's about sexual abuse. But I am scared. This male-dominated society will tear me apart. But your words have given me strength. What do you think? Should I write it?'

'Of course you should! If you are inspired, who can hold you back?'

As we were talking, Jayatha began to shiver. Her teeth chattered. I, too, was feeling very cold. Suddenly Jayatha stopped. She grabbed me with both arms and hugged me tight.

'I can't bear this cold. Hold me tight!' Jayatha spoke through her chattering teeth.

For a moment, I became wary. A sweeping glance reassured me that nobody was around. Then, I felt ashamed of myself. This living body had come close to me in search of warmth, so why was I so full of misgivings? I gently removed her arms from around me and took hold of her hands. I rubbed them, I massaged them, and, putting my arm round her shoulder, I drew her close. I said, 'Forget about your phone call. Let's go back. Walk briskly. You will feel better once you're inside.'

Like an obedient child, Jayatha began to walk. She shivered in the cold; I quickened my pace. We didn't say a word until we had reached the guesthouse. When we reached her door, I said, 'Now go into your room and warm yourself by the heater.'

'Please come in with me. I don't feel like staying alone,' Jayatha said in a plaintive voice.

'Don't be silly, Jayatha! You know very well that it's

not right for me to come into your room, particularly at this hour.'

'In that case, I will come to *your* room. Please don't leave me here alone!'

'Okay. In that case, I will wake your uncle up. He'll keep you company.'

'No! No! I'd rather die!' she exclaimed as she marched into her room and slammed the door shut.

That night, I could not sleep for a very long time. Was she just a simple, naïve girl or was she putting on a clever act? Was it a mistake to have ignored Jalappa's warning? How do I look at her? As a creative young writer or as a model for a character in some future story of mine? Or, am I supporting her perverseness?

Returning from my morning walk the next day, I saw her standing in her doorway, sipping a cup of tea.

'Good morning, Manohar!' she greeted me pleasantly.

'Good morning, Jayatha. The late riser seems to have got up early this morning!'

'I didn't get up. I just didn't sleep the whole night!' she remarked with a laugh.

As I was unlocking my door she said, 'Manohar, call out to me when you're going for breakfast.' She went back into her room without waiting for a reply.

After a shower and a shave, I browsed through the morning paper. After reading my notes, I put on my clothes. I opened the door to leave when I saw Mrs Saklani shutting Jayatha's door and looking around, bewildered. She was muttering something as she got out. Noticing me, she said in a disgusted tone, 'This woman! She is so...'

'Why? What happened?'

'Since I'm leaving today, I thought I'd say bye to her. Finding the door open, I knocked and went in looking for her... Never mind; forget it, okay! My train leaves this morning. Bye then, Manohar.' And Mrs Saklani was gone.

I glanced at Jayatha's room and shrugged. I had breakfast with Vikram and Jalappa. As we were getting up, Jayatha walked in.

'Please keep me company. Sit with me till I finish, please!'

This was too much!

'Sorry, Jayatha! We've finished our breakfast. You carry on,' I said as we left.

Jayatha followed us out. Vikram asked her, 'What happened, Jayatha? Aren't you having any breakfast?'

'Forget it. Going without breakfast for one day is not going to kill me!'

Everybody was stumped. I was annoyed, but I also felt sorry for her. 'Okay then, I will keep you company.' I went back into the canteen with her.

'You're going too far, Jayatha. You're trying to blackmail me!'

'No problem. All is fair in love!'

That left me stunned. Just then, her uncle walked into the mess and sat at a table.

'Doesn't he talk to you?'

'Of course he does! He was just telling me that he saw

us both coming back together late yesterday and the day before. He said that since you were quite elderly, he did not make an issue of it. Otherwise, he wouldn't have let me even go out.'

I just remembered Mrs Saklani and how flustered she appeared. 'What happened to Mrs Saklani this morning?'

Jayatha collapsed into gales of laughter. She laughed so much that she almost choked. Even the mess-boy stopped to look. I offered her a tumbler of water.

'It was really funny! I had gone for a bath. I must have left the room door open. The bathroom door, too, was ajar. I had just soaped myself when she came in. Because I wasn't in the room, she poked her head into the bathroom—and then! She almost screamed!'

I was dumbfounded by her candour and said nothing.

When we reached the coach, Jayatha said, 'Today is the last day of the seminar. What shall we do tomorrow?'

'We? I will be going to my cousin's house today.'

'You won't come sightseeing tomorrow?'

'No. I've seen it all.'

Jayatha was silent for a long time. All at once, she held my hand and said in a pleading voice, 'Please, let's spend just one day together!'

Freeing my hand, I said, 'Jayatha, behave yourself!'

'If I behave myself, will you stay?'

I couldn't help but laugh. I said, 'No. My cousin will come to collect me this evening. I have to go.'

'So when will we meet again?'

'Come to Goa. And bring your husband along, too.'

She smiled for a brief moment. 'I have stopped dreaming.'

'In that case, if I happen to come to Chennai, I will come to your place.'

'I can't invite you to my place. Nobody would approve of it.'

She paused, and then asked, 'Will you remember me?'

'I don't easily forget my friends. What about you?'

Without answering my question, she asked, 'How do you eat chocolate? Do you eat it quickly or do you savour it?'

'I savour it, of course.'

'I chew it fast. I love to enjoy anything immediately. I doubt that you have ever knocked mangoes off a tree. I guess you'd rather wait till they ripen and fall on their own!'

I was becoming distinctly uncomfortable at the direction the conversation was taking. Just then, Balraj came by and I excused myself.

The seminar concluded early, at four in the evening. Bidding goodbye to one another, everybody dispersed. The organizers had arranged a sightseeing tour of Delhi and Agra the following day. Those who were visiting Delhi for the first time stayed back.

Umesh came to collect me and I went to my room to get my suitcase. When I came out, Jayatha was blocking my way. 'You are cheating!' she remarked angrily.

'Hi, Jayatha! Say goodbye with a smile please. Umesh, this is my writer friend Jayatha.'

'So, you'll be staying with him. Could you give me your phone number, please? You never know when it will come handy.' And, before I could open my mouth, Umesh gave it to her.

On the way, I told Umesh about Jayatha.

'In that case, you will definitely get a call from her tomorrow!'

'Why tomorrow? I'll get a call today itself, you'll see!'

But no call came that night. Perhaps she did not find the right person to accompany her to the phone booth.

The call came early the next morning. 'Hello, Manohar! I miss you!'

'Just for a day or two. After that you will forget me.' And, before she could say anything further, I continued, 'You're going sightseeing today. Have a nice time.'

'I'm not in the mood to go. But Uncle is quite enthusiastic.' She prattled on till I disconnected.

I was taking a small nap after lunch when she phoned again. 'I am lost here in Vrindavan. As I was walking in Krishna's Vrindavan, I lost my way. After finally getting back, I discovered that the coach had gone off, leaving me stranded!'

Hearing Jayatha's pitiful voice, sleep fled my eyes. 'Calm down, Jayatha. You're not in a foreign country. The coach won't go away without you. Wait there; it will come back for you.' I spoke confidently, but I was worried.

'Please, Manohar. Come fetch me,' Jayatha was pleading.

'That won't be possible, Jayatha. But don't worry. Wait

there for an hour or so and, if nobody comes, take a bus or cab back to Delhi. If you have any problem, give me a call.'

There was no call after that. Had it come, I would have felt relief.

Just as I was waking up the next morning, the call came. 'I'm leaving now. Please come to meet me!'

'What happened yesterday? How did you return?'

'The coach came back for me.'

'You should have phoned and told me so. I was worried.'

'You were worried about me? I'm so happy!'

Damn this woman! I was about to hang up the phone in exasperation when Jayatha repeated, 'Please come to the station.'

'You must be crazy! I, too, am going back today. I have to catch the ten o'clock flight.'

'In that case, come to the station and meet me on your way to the airport. Please!'

I prevaricated, 'Okay, I'll try to come.'

I didn't go, of course.

Jayatha had excited my literary instincts. I had been tickled, and pinched, and I could feel the bruise. I must write a story on Jayatha, I resolved.

But there is a wide gulf between decision and execution. A year and a half went by. The Tamil Sangh of Goa had invited the renowned writer, Professor Jayakrishnan, as their chief guest for some function. He phoned to say that he was in Goa. I invited him over for lunch. After lunch, we sat talking. I suddenly remembered Jayatha. When I asked if he had heard of her, he nodded, saying, 'Yes, I have read her. She writes very well.'

I was pleased. I said, 'I've heard her famous story about the doll. Very beautiful.'

'Which one is that?'

I told him the gist of the story in a few words.

'You must be mistaken. It's an excellent story, no doubt, but it is not Jayatha's. It is a widely acclaimed story from Pramila's pen.'

'Are you sure?'

'Of course I'm sure! I teach the story to my college students.'

'Could this Jayatha be a fraud?'

'I don't know her personally, but she writes very well. I've recently read a new story of hers. It's about an episode involving her encounter with an aging Lothario of a writer.'

I became alert. 'Can you give me the synopsis of the story, please?'

'Her writing is usually slightly erotic and indiscreet. This one is written in the first person. About how, when she went for a seminar, an elderly writer tries to befriend her, dogging her footsteps throughout the seminar. How he seeks her company every night, under the pretext of making phone calls. How he holds her hand, using the cold as an excuse. How he opens her bathroom door and peeks in while she's having a shower. And how he hugs her on the last day of the seminar, claiming that he was shivering from the cold! And, when she could not bear it any longer, how she shoved him away, forcing him to leave the guesthouse. And how, on the last day, he shamelessly comes to see her off at the station, where she gives him a piece of her mind! She has ended it very well.'

I was left speechless.

Translator's Note

The stories in this collection were written over a period of more than four decades—from the mid-sixties of the last century to until the end of the last decade of this century. 'For Death Does Not Come' was written when Mauzo was a college student in Bombay. 'Bandh', written in 1987, was published after the Post-Liberation Konkani Language Agitation of which Mauzo was a front-ranking leader. 'In the Land of Humans' and 'Happy Birthday' were written in 2009.

The present-day reader may find it difficult to envision 'a four-anna tot of feni' which was, even then, paid for with a twenty-five-paise coin. That very coin has now been demonetized! In the title story, 'Teresa's Man', set in the early seventies, we find that travelling double-seat on a cycle was a common mode of transport—something the modern generation, where even kids ride to school on motorized two-wheelers, would find laughable. Those were the days of steam engined-trains, kerosene lamps, very few cars, low salaries, no televisions or computers, when even phones were a rarity. Accounts were then still toted in annas which, though demonetized by then, still had a lot of purchasing power. The Goa of then, especially South Goa where almost all the stories are set, had the two major communities, Hindus and Catholics, living side by side in harmony. The village church bells regularly tolled at Noon and Angelus, at dusk—not only calls to prayer but a timekeeper when few people had watches. All in all, a world that, today, is a distant memory.